# Dick Wh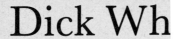

## A Pantomime

John Crocker

Lyrics and Music by
Eric Gilder

© 1967 By John Crocker and Eric Gilder

Samuel French–London
New York–Sydney–Toronto–Hollywood

## PRODUCTION NOTE

Pantomime, as we know it today, is a form of entertainment all on its own, derived from a number of different sources - the commedia dell' arte (and all that that derived from), the ballet, the opera, the music hall and the realms of folk-lore and fairy tale. And elements of all of these are still to be found in it. This strange mixture has created a splendid topsy-turvy world where men are women, women are men, where the present is embraced within the past, where people are hit but not hurt, where authority is constantly flouted, where fun is poked at everything including pantomime itself at times, and, above all, where magic abounds and dreams invariably come true. In other words, it is - or should be - fun. Fun to do and fun to watch and the sense of enjoyment which can be conveyed by a cast is very important to the enjoyment of the audience.

Pantomime can be very simply staged if resources are limited. Basically a tab surround at the back, tab legs at the sides and a set of traverse tabs for the frontcloth scenes, together with the simplest of small cut-out pieces to suggest the various locales (or even just placards with this information written on them) will suffice. Conversely, there is no limit to the extent to which more lavish facilities can be employed.

The directions I have given in the text adopt a middle course and are based on a permanent setting of a cyclorama skycloth at the back, a few feet in front of which is a rostrum about two feet high, running the width of the stage. About two thirds of the depth downstage is a false proscenium, immediately behind which are the lines for the set of traverse table. Below the false proscenium are arched entrances left and right, with possible one foot reveals to the proscenium. A border will be necessary at some point between the false proscenium and the cyclorama to mask lighting battens and the top of the cyclorama. Lastly, there is a set of steps leading from the front of the stage into the auditorium, which I have referred to as the catwalk. I have imagined it to be set stage left, but it is unimportant whether it is left or right.

Into this permanent setting are placed various wings left and right, (I have catered for one a side set on a level with the border, but a greater depth of stage may require two a side for masking purposes). Cut-out ground rows set on the front or back of the rostrum complete the full sets. On smaller stages these cut-outs seen against the cyclorama give a better impression of depth than backcloths. The frontcloth fly lines come in behind the traverse tabs. Cloths can, of course, be tumbled or rolled if flying space is limited. It is a good tip always to bring in the traverse tabs when a cloth has to be lowered, then if any hitch occurs the lights can still come up and the actors get on with the scene. Similarly, I have indicated where the traverse tabs should be closed in frontcloth scenes, so that there is plenty of time for the cloth to be flown before the end of the scene. The quick flow of one scene into the next is important if a smooth running production is to be achieved.

The settings and costumes should preferably be in clear bright colours to give a story book effect. The Mediaeval period is, of course, most suited to 'Dick Whittington', but deliberate anachronisms should be introduced into some settings and some of the comics' costumes. JACK's sailor trousers for Scene 8 will need to be specially made. They should be as generous as possible round the waist and gathered in on a strong elastic waistband. Animal skins can be hired from Theatre Zoo, 28 New Row, London WC2.

Pantomime requires many props and often they will have to be home made. Instructions are given in the prop plot about any of the more awkward seeming ones. Props should also be colourfully painted and in pantomime most props should be much larger than reality. It is also wise for the property master to examine carefully the practical use to which a prop is to be put - it is very painful to be hit with a giant's club of solid wood, one of material filled with foam plastic is far gentler!

I have not attempted to give a lighting plot as this entirely depends on the equipment available, but, generally speaking, most pantomime lighting needs to be full up, warm and bright. Pinks and ambers are probably best for this, but a circuit of blues in the cyclorama battens will help nightfall and dawn rising effects.

Follow spots are a great help for this kind of show, but not essential. But, if they are available, it is often effective in romantic numbers to fade out the stage lighting and hold the principals in the follow spots, quickly fading up on the last few bars because this can help to increase the applause! They can also be used for the FAIRY and DEMON to give them greater freedom of movement than with fixed front of house or spot-bar spots.

Flash boxes, with the necessary colour and flash powders, can be obtained from the usual stage electrical suppliers.

The music has been specially composed so that it is easy for the less musically accomplished to master, but it is also scored in parts for the more ambitious. If an orchestra is available, well and good, but a single piano will suffice. It is an advantage, however, if there can be a drummer as well. Not only because a rhythm accompaniment enhances the numbers, but also because, for some reason never yet fully fathomed, slapstick hits and falls are always twice as funny if they coincide with a well timed bonk on a drum, wood-block or whatever is found to make the noise best suited to the action. A drummer can also cope with the various 'whizzes' and 'tings' noted in the directions, though, if necessary, they can, of course, be done off stage. A special type of whistle can be got for the 'whizz', and the 'ting' requires a triangle.

Pantomime demands a particular style of playing and production. The acting must be larger than life, but still sincere, with a good deal of sparkle and attack. Much of it must be projected directly at the audience, since one of pantomime's great advantages is that it deliberately breaks down the 'fourth wall'. The actors can literally and metaphorically shake hands with their audience who become almost another member of the cast; indeed, their active participation from time to time is essential. A word of warning, though, on this - the actors must always remain in control; for instance, if a demon or villain encourages hissing, he must make sure it is never to such an extent that he can no longer be heard. The producer should see that the story line is clearly brought out and treated with respect. There is always room for local gags and topical quips in pantomime, but they should not be overdone. Most important of all, the comedy, as any comedy, must never appear to be conscious of its own funniness.

Characterization should be very clear and definite. I prefer the traditional use of a man to play the Dame and a girl to play the Principal Boy. In the case of the Dame, anyway, there is a sound argument for this - audiences will laugh more readily at a man impersonating a woman involved in the mock cruelties of slapstick than at a real woman. For this reason an actor playing a Dame should never quite let us forget he is a man, while giving a sincere character performance of a woman; further, he can be as feminine as he likes, but never effeminate. SARAH is full of boisterous good nature which seldom fails her in any circumstances.

A Principal Boy also requires a character performance, but, of course, with the implications reversed! An occasional slap of the thigh is not sufficient. DICK should be a particularly boyish Boy. His outlook is romantic and he has to show considerable courage in the face of many reverses.

Principal Girls can be a bore, but only if they are presented as mere pretty symbols of feminine sweetness. ALICE has a gay disposition, but is fully aware of the practicalities of life.

Her father, ALDERMAN FITZWARREN, tends to bumble his way through life. His short-sightedness, after all, only allows him a very hazy view of what is happening around him.

His apprentice, IDLE JACK, in spite of his 'framing' of DICK, is without malice. It is a part in which the actor playing him can to some extent exploit his own personality.

The CAPTAIN is a natural leader in that all he does naturally leads to failure. The MATE, if he is even aware of this, is fully resigned to it; indeed, he is more at home with failure than success.

FAIRY SILVERCHIME and KING RAT need playing with great spirit and with great conviction of the rightness of their own causes.

PRINCESS ULUL should look very attractive but be innocently unaware of it. She should also have some ability as a comedienne.

Her father, the EMPEROR, has an easy-going manner providing everything goes as he wishes, for he is obviously used to being obeyed without question.

His guards and attendants are all very Eastern and very subservient to their master.

TOMMY, the cat, is unusually loyal for a cat, but is very catlike in every other way - self sufficient, sharply intelligent and with a highly realistic approach to life.

THOMASINA is, as it were, a sex-kitten.

The number of CHORUS used can be as many or as few as desired.

John Crocker

This play is fully protected under the copyright laws of the British Commonwealth of Nations, the United States of America, and all countries of the Berne and Universal Copyright Conventions.

All right are strictly reserved.

It is an infringement of the copyright to give any public performance or reading of this play either in its entirety or in the form of excerpts without the prior consent of the copyright owners. No part of this publication may be transmitted, stored in a retrieval system, or reproduced in any form or by any means, electronic, mechanical, photocopying, manuscript, typescript, recording, or otherwise, without the prior permission of the copyright owners.

SAMUEL FRENCH LTD, 26 SOUTHAMPTON STREET, STRAND, LONDON WC2E 7JE, or their authorized agents, issue licences to amateurs to give performances of this play on payment of a fee. **This fee is subject to contract and subject to variation at the sole discretion of Samuel French Ltd.**

Licences are issued subject to the understanding that it shall be made clear in all advertising matter that the audience will witness an amateur performance; and that the names of the authors of the plays shall be included on all announcements and on all programmes.

**The publication of this play must not be taken to imply that it is necessarily available for performance by amateurs or professionals,** either in the British Isles or overseas. Amateurs intending production must, in their own interests, make application to Samuel French Ltd or their authorized agents, for consent before starting rehearsals or booking a theatre or hall.

ISBN 0 573 06465 2

## CHARACTERS

| | |
|---|---|
| ALDERMAN FITZWARREN | |
| IDLE JACK | – his apprentice |
| ALICE | – his daughter |
| SARAH | – his cook |
| KING RAT | |
| FAIRY SILVERCHIME | |
| TOMMY | – the cat |
| DICK WHITTINGTON | |
| CUTTLE | – the captain (of the 'Saucy Sal') |
| and | |
| SCUTTLE | – his mate |
| PRINCESS ULUL OF MOROCCO | |
| CASSIM* | – captain of the Moroccan Guard |
| ABDUL* | |
| FAKRASH* | – guards |
| ALI* | |
| THE EMPEROR OF MOROCCO | |
| MUSTAPHA* | – his attendant |
| THOMASINA* | – a lady cat |

(*Chorus parts)

CHORUS as citizens, apprentices, fairies, sailors, harem wives, etc.

### SYNOPSIS OF SCENES
#### Part I

| | |
|---|---|
| Scene 1 | Aldgate |
| Scene 2 | Petticoat Lane |
| Scene 3 | Fitzwarren's Stores |
| Scene 4 | On the way to Highgate Hill |
| Scene 5 | Highgate Hill |

#### Part II

| | |
|---|---|
| Scene 6 | The Docks at Wapping |
| Scene 7 | 'Tween Decks |
| Scene 8 | The Main Deck of the 'Saucy Sal' |
| Scene 9 | The Shores of Morocco |
| Scene 10 | The Emperor of Morocco's Palace |
| Scene 11 | Back in London |
| Scene 12 | Sir Richard Whittington's Reception at the Guildhall |

MUSIC 1  Overture

PART I

Scene One - ALDGATE

(Full set. Cut-out ground row of Mediaeval London streets along back of rostrum. U.C. in front of rostrum a pump, labelled 'YE OLDE ALDGATE PUMP', with cup attached on a chain. Inn piece R. with sign 'YE OLDE ALDGATE BEER PUMP' and with a practical door. Shop piece L., 'FITZWARREN'S STORES', with practical door, fitted with bell pull and a knocker.
CHORUS, as citizens and apprentices, discovered singing and dancing Opening Chorus.

MUSIC 2  'LONDON' words by John Crocker, music 'Oranges and Lemons' arranged by Eric Gilder.)

CHORUS
London, oh, London,
Oh, glorious London!
Hear the bells ringing,
All London is singing -
From Broad Street and Aldgate
To Hampstead and Highgate -
For London so gay
Is on holiday!

The people come dancing,
The horses come prancing;
The butcher, the baker,
the candle-stick maker,
The glover, the tinsmith,
The draper, the goldsmith,
Like us they will go
To the Lord Mayor's Show.

(Dance.)

London, oh, London,
Oh, glorious London!
Hear the bells ringing,
All London is singing -
From Broad Street and Aldgate
To Hampstead and Highgate,
From Bankside and Blackfriars
To Westcheap and Whitefriars -
For London so gay
Is on holiday!   Yes, on holiday!

(ALDERMAN FITZWARREN, wearing spectacles, appears in his shop doorway.)

**FITZWARREN** Good morning, townsfolk.

**CHORUS** Good morning, Alderman Fitzwarren.

**FITZWARREN** Lovely day, is - (He moves forward and trips and falls over one of CHORUS, who is kneeling down, losing his glasses.) Who left that dog there? Now I've lost me specs. Where are me specs? (Takes a second pair from pocket and puts them on to look for others.)

**1st CHORUS** You've just put them on, Mr Fitzwarren.

**FITZWARREN** Well, of course I have. I couldn't see to find 'em if I wasn't wearing 'em, could I? Ah, there they are. (Finds first pair and puts them on over others.) That's better, now I can see properly. (Looking at back of head of one of CHORUS.) Blimey, you need a shave, my boy. I say, you all look very happy this morning.

**2nd CHORUS** Well, today's Lord Mayor's day.

**3rd CHORUS** And Lord Mayor's day is a holiday.

**FITZWARREN** Good gracious, so it is. I expect you'll all have lots of money to spend. I must get me shop opened at once. (Calling into shop.) Idle Jack! Idle Jack! (Slight pause.) Idle Jack! (To CHORUS.) Any of you seen Jack today?

**CHORUS** No, Mr Fitzwarren.

**FITZWARREN** Tt, tt, that boy's never here when there's any work to be done.

(Loud snoring and whistling off R.)

What's that?

(Louder snoring and whistling.)

**CHORUS** (looking off R.) It's Jack!

(MUSIC 3 IDLE JACK enters U.R., his eyes closed and his arms stretched out before him sleep-walking. Round his neck hangs a notice, 'DO NOT DISTURB', and from his waist a large prop alarm clock is suspended.)

**4th CHORUS** He's walking in his sleep.

**FITZWARREN** Well, he's always been a bit of a day dreamer. We must wake him up.

**CHORUS** (shouting) Jack, wake up!

**FITZWARREN** Ssh! Not like that. You might give him a shock and shocks are very dangerous to sleepwalkers. We must only shout in a whisper. Like this -

(Follows on behind JACK, who is circling stage slowly anti-clockwise. Whispering.)

Jack, wake up!

**CHORUS** (following on behind FITZWARREN, each shout getting louder) Jack, wake up! Jack, wake up! JACK, WAKE UP! JACK, WAKE UP!

(FITZWARREN and CHORUS stop.)

**FITZWARREN** Hm, he doesn't seem to hear whispers. We must think of something else that's not noisy.

(JACK reaches D.C. and his alarm clock starts to ring loudly, EFFECT 1. Bell off. He stops, yawning and stretching. CHORUS put their hands to their ears and FITZWARREN runs round in short-sighted circles shouting above the noise.)

What's that? Stop it! It's too noisy! It'll give him a shock!   (Lands beside JACK.)   Oh, it's you, Jack.

**JACK** (shouting) No, it's not me. It's my alarm clock. It's ringing.

**FITZWARREN** (shouting) Stop it!

**JACK** Oh, righto.   (Takes a prop hammer from pocket and hits clock. Ringing stops and large spring flies out of top, catch released by JACK.)

**FITZWARREN** I didn't mean stop it working altogether.

**JACK** Oh, that's only the mainspring.   (Throws clock off.)

**FITZWARREN** Tcha! Now come along, Jack. It's high time we opened the shop. There's not much for you to do; just sweep the floors, dust the counters, pat the butter, string the sausages, fillet the fish, dress the crabs, pot the paste and dash the habery.

(JACK has been drooping at each successive task and now faints. FITZWARREN turns and bumps into flat beside shop door.)

Who moved that door?   (He exits into shop.)

(JACK sits up.)

JACK Pat the fish, butter the counters, sweep the sausages. I can't waste my time with all that work. My mind is on higher things than work.

5th CHORUS What things?

JACK (blissfully)   Love.

(CHORUS laugh.)

I'm in love with old Fitzy's daughter, Alice, and I'm trying to think of something wonderful I can do to win her.

5th CHORUS You'll never do anything wonderful, Jack. You're too lazy.

1st CHORUS Yes, you're always falling asleep.

(JACK falls asleep on his feet.)

CHORUS Jack, wake up!

JACK (wakes)   Did I fall asleep? Oh dear, that always happens if someone talks about sleep. And I need a lot of people to wake me. It's lucky you were all here. But supposing you weren't - what could I do then?

(2nd CHORUS whispers in JACK's ear.)

What? Ask them?

(He indicates Audience, 2nd CHORUS nods.)

Do you think they would?

(2nd CHORUS nods again.)

Well, I'll try.   (To Audience.)   I say, if you

see me falling asleep like this – (Demonstrates.)
Would you wake me up? (Reaction.)
I couldn't quite hear. Would you? (Reaction.)
Good, let's practice it then. Whenever you see me
do this – (Demonstrates.) you shout,
'Jack, wake up!' Ready? Right. (Pretends to
fall asleep.)

(CHORUS encourage Audience to shout.)

Have you shouted yet? We'd better try again,
then. (Falls asleep.)

(CHORUS encourage Audience.)

Ah, that's better but sometimes I'm very fast
asleep. See if you can do it a bit louder. (Falls
asleep.)

(CHORUS encourage Audience.)

Ah, that's it! It's not that I'm really lazy, you
know. In fact, I'm a very busy little fellow.

(MUSIC 4 'BUSY LITTLE FELLOW')

I'm a busy little fellow in an awful plight,
'Cos they always keep me working from the morn
    till night.
They even keep me busy while the moon's above,
So I've hardly even had the time to fall in love.
I'm always very busy and I never stop for tea.
I'm in such an awful tizzy that I don't know if I'm me!
I am hurrying as slowly as a fellow can –
Oh, who would be apprentice to an Alderman?

**CHORUS**    He is hurrying as slowly as a fellow can –
Oh, who would be apprentice to an Alderman?

**JACK**    Jar the jam and dust the ham
And dress the mutton up as lamb;
Don't let the carving knife get blunt
And put the ripest fruit in front.
I'm very conscientious and I work myself to death,
And yet they never even give me time to take
    another breath!
I am hurrying as slowly as a fellow can –
Oh, who would be apprentice to an Alderman?

| | |
|---|---|
| CHORUS | He is hurrying as slowly as a fellow can - Oh, who would be apprentice to an Alderman? |
| JACK | Put some sugar in the sand And give the errand boy a hand, And if I ever stop to talk The gorgonzola wants its walk. The things that people want are always on the highest shelves, And I should like to tell them they can do the bloomin' job themselves! I'm a busy little fellow in an awful plight, 'Cos they always keep me working from the morn till night, |
| CHORUS | He is hurrying as slowly as a fellow can - |
| JACK and CHORUS | Oh, who would be apprentice to an Alderman! (Exit JACK into shop.) |
| | (MUSIC 5  Enter ALICE FITZWARREN U.R.) |
| CHORUS | Hullo, Alice. |
| ALICE | Hullo, boys and girls. Isn't it a lovely day? I've just been to see all the decorations for the Lord Mayor's Show. |
| | (Enter FITZWARREN from shop wearing bowler hat.) |
| FITZWARREN | Alice! Alice, where art thou? (Looks round vaguely and stops beside her.) Have any of you seen my daughter? |
| ALICE | I'm here, father. |
| FITZWARREN | (peering closely at her)   What? Oh, so you are. I've got to go out, my dear. Keep an eye on Jack, will you? He's just started work and he'll stop again if someone doesn't keep him at it. |
| ALICE | Don't you think you ought to get another apprentice as well as Jack, father, to sort of make up for him? |
| FITZWARREN | Yes, but it would cost me another lot of wages. Still, I tell you what - I'll think the idea over for a long time till you've forgotten it and then I won't mention it again - I can't say fairer than that, can I? |

Now I was just off to the Guildhall. I was invited there for elevenses at tenses. (Takes large prop hour glass from pocket.) Good heavenses, it is tenses! Now I shan't be there in time if I don't leave fifteen minutes ago. (Hurries U.C., putting hour glass away and bumps into pump.) Oops! (Raising bowler to it.) Beg pardon, madam. (Exit U.L.)

ALICE  Poor father, he's so shortsighted and he won't spend any money on a new pair of glasses. I wish he'd spend some on a new apprentice, though.

CHORUS  Why?

ALICE  Well, you never know, we might get a very handsome new apprentice and I should like that. If he was very, very handsome, then perhaps I'd fall in love with him. I'd rather like to fall in love today.

(MUSIC 6  'I'D LIKE TO FALL IN LOVE')

There's lots of things I'd like to do
   This lovely day in Spring.
Like climbing up an apple tree
   Or hearing blackbirds sing.
But though I'd like to stand on my head,
   And kick my heels above,
The thing I'd like to do the best -
   I'd like to fall in love!

I know plenty of things to do;
Just as many, I'm sure, as you;
But I wish I were kissing now.
Please won't somebody show me how?

There's lots of things I'd like to do
   This lovely day in Spring.
Like climbing up an apple tree
   Or hearing blackbirds sing.
But though I'd like to stand on my head,
   And kick my heels above,
The thing I'd like to do the best -
   I'd like to fall in love!

(Exit ALICE into shop and CHORUS variously.

1 - 1 - 8

|||
|---|---|
| | Hooting and <u>EFFECT 2.</u>  Very loud car engine heard off R.) |
| SARAH | (off R.)   Stop! Stop! Come back here! Stop! |
| | (MUSIC 7   Enter SARAH U.R., apparently dragged on by a wheeled shopping basket fitted with a prop engine, which she tries to guide by its walking stick handle. On the front of the basket is a large card with the letters 'V.L.' Numerous parcels piled in the basket scatter as she enters and pursues an erratic course round the stage until the basket brakes to a sudden stop D.C. and SARAH, still holding the handle, is carried past it by her own momentum till she can go no further and falls backwards.) |
| | Well, really! And me a Veteran Learner too. (Rises, rubbing behind painfully.)   Ooh, me bottom gear will never be the same again. I wonder if it's quietened down?   (Tentatively touches it, draws hand quickly away and tries again.)   Yes, it's all right.   (Grasps handle firmly and basket shoots forward and off L. with a burst of noise, <u>EFFECT 3,</u> landing her flat on her face. She rises painfully.)   Oh dear, now it's given me a nasty jolt in a built up area. I must apologise for it behaving like that. I do hope it didn't wake any of you up. Well, how d'ye do? (Curtsies.)   My name is Sarah. I'm Alderman Fitzwarren's cook. I've just been out doing the shopping and - oh! Look at all me parcels. (Collects parcels together and picks one up.) Now, what's this?   (Rattles it, holding her ear to it.)   Oh dear, the eggs. Scrambled again. (Throws parcel off L. and picks up remainder, by holding up the front edges of her skirt and placing them in the bag thus made. Turns toward Audience, which displays her underwear.) |
| CONDUCTOR | Hey, Sarah, your skirt! |
| SARAH | What's the matter with me skirt?   (Peers over edge of it and realises.)   Ooh!   (Very embarrassed, crouches down and shuffles over to shop and throws parcels off, then straightens up |

still holding skirt.) I am a silly girl.
(Realises she is still holding skirt and hurriedly
drops it.) Oh! (To CONDUCTOR.)
Thank you for pointing out my slip, Charlie (or
whatever his name is) - I mean, the one I made,
not the one I'm wearing. (To Audience.)
Have you met Charlie? He's the one in the middle
here. You can pick him out quite easily because
every time the others play some music he stands
up and does his exercises. Still, he's very nice.
But I mustn't stay here gossiping all day, I must
get on with me work, though I do love a gossip.
Well, I always say a good gossip keeps you young,
and if you keep young, you won't grow old, will
you? Anyway, I think the thing is to -

(MUSIC 8 'AS YOUNG AS YOU THINK'. Words and
Music by John Crocker.)

Be as young as you think you are
And not as old as you feel,
Say to yourself - in the pink you are!
And years from your age it will steal.
Be as young as you think you are,
That's my motto anyway, hey!
    Life is short but sweet,
      Give yourself a treat,
And grow younger ev'ry day.

(Dance.)

Be as young as you feel you are,
It's not as old as you think
Say to yourself - it's ideal you are!
And years will drop off in a wink.
Be as young as you feel you are,
That's my motto anyway, hey!
    Life's too short to cry,
      Live before you die,
And grow younger ev'ry day,
   Yes, really -
You'll grow younger ev'ry day!

(Exit into Shop. LIGHTS DIM. MUSIC 9. GREEN
FLASH L. and GREEN SPOT UP as KING RAT enters
there.)

KING RAT	Now let all joy and laughter cease,
King Rat doth bid thee, hold thy peace!
And list while I unfold a scheme
That shall bring true my fondest dream.
To London comes a youth today,
Who's guarded by a pesky fay –
A certain Fairy Silverchime
That hath held sway too long a time –
But now her overthrow I've plann'd
Wherein this youth shall lend a hand,
For he – Dick Whittington by name –
I'll ruin and then use his shame
To undermine the Fairy's pow'r
And gain my most triumphant hour!

(Laughs fiendishly. **MUSIC 10.** WHITE SPOT UP R. and FAIRY SILVERCHIME enters into it.)

SILVERCHIME	Not so, King Rat, ye never will
While I can guard against such ill!
Ye are discovered in your crime!

KING RAT	Confound it! Fairy Silverchime!

SILVERCHIME	Thy boast of triumph comes too soon,
I bring my ward a priceless boon
Which shall thy evil scheming thwart.

KING RAT	Indeed! What is this 'boon' ye've brought?

SILVERCHIME	Thy direst enemy, King Rat,
The foe of all thy kind – a cat!

KING RAT	(aside)    Confusion! 'Twill my plans delay.
(to her)    A murrain on thee, meddling fay!
Nathless, though ye may well begin,
I shall the final battle win!    (Exits L.)

SILVERCHIME	His words are barren as the air,
In deeds 'tis little fruit they'll bear.
But one awaits.

TOMMY	(off R.)    Meow!

SILVERCHIME	                Come forth, good cat.

(**MUSIC 11**    TOMMY bounds on R.)

And welcome.

1 - 1 - 11

| | |
|---|---|
| TOMMY | (rises on hind paws and bows low. Then scents something and crosses to where KING RAT stood and pads around, arching back and sniffing hard.) |
| SILVERCHIME | Ah, you smell a rat. |
| TOMMY | (nods agreement and begins to follow scent off L.) |
| SILVERCHIME | Nay - ye for now must leave him free; Soon thy new master here will be. Now dost remember all my words? |
| TOMMY | (ponders, scratching head, then nods. EFFECT 4. A bird is heard singing off L. He jumps up and runs towards noise.) |
| SILVERCHIME | I nothing said of chasing birds. |
| TOMMY | (returns sheepishly, then holds up one paw and smacks it with the other ) |
| SILVERCHIME | Ye are forgiven, never fear. |
| TOMMY | (affectionately rubs himself against her legs) |
| SILVERCHIME | But now 'tis time to leave thee here; I prithee, in thy task excel.<br><br>(MUSIC 12. DICK is heard singing off L.)<br><br>Hark! There's thy master - |
| TOMMY | (cups a paw to his ear then looks off L. Gives face a quick cat lick and whiskers a twirl) |
| SILVERCHIME | So farewell.<br><br>(Exit FAIRY R. TOMMY waves goodbye and runs to hide behind pump. Enter DICK WHITTINGTON L. singing a few bars of his song to bring him to C. and, of course, carrying a bundle on a stick on his shoulder.) |
| DICK | Well, here I am at last in London Town; and just in time to see the Lord Mayor's Show. One day I hope to be Lord Mayor myself, but it's going to be difficult without anyone to help me. London's such a big place and everybody seems so unfriendly. (Sees inn.) Gosh, I'm thirsty - I don't think I can afford to buy a drink, though. (Sees pump.) |

|         |                                                                                                                                      |
|---------|--------------------------------------------------------------------------------------------------------------------------------------|
|         | Never mind, this is free.   (Pumps a drink into cup attached to pump and drinks.)   That's better. |
| TOMMY   | (comes from behind pump and rubs himself against DICK's legs)   Meow. |
| DICK    | (stroking him)   Hullo, puss. You seem friendly, anyway. Would you like a drink, too? |
| TOMMY   | (nods) |
| DICK    | (pumping drink)   I'm afraid it's only water - they don't have pumps with milk.<br><br>(Holds out cup, which TOMMY laps from.)<br><br>I wonder who you belong to? |
| TOMMY   | (points to DICK) |
| DICK    | To me? |
| TOMMY   | (nods decidedly) |
| DICK    | Well, I'd like to be your master and if you really want to stay with me I shall be very pleased to have you. |
| TOMMY   | (nods and holds out R. paw) |
| DICK    | That's settled it, eh?   (Laughs and shakes the paw.)   Now, what shall I call you? |
| TOMMY   | (ponders a minute, scratching head, then with a paw traces TOMMY in the air) |
| DICK    | (spelling out the letters as they are made) T O M M Y. |
| TOMMY   | (puts in a full stop) |
| DICK    | (laughs)   Tommy, eh? |
| TOMMY   | (nods) |
| DICK    | I must say, you're a very clever cat, Tommy. |
| TOMMY   | (heartily agrees) |
| DICK    | (laughs)   Well, if I'm to win my fortune I shall need somebody clever around. Do you know, they told me at home the streets of London were paved with gold. Gold! All the pavements I've trodden so far have been made of stone - and very hard |

stone at that. Never mind, maybe winning a fortune isn't going to be easy, but I've a feeling that with you to help me I'll manage it somehow.

(MUSIC 13 'SOMETHING'S BOUND TO HAPPEN')

Something's bound to happen when the skies are blue,
Something's bound to happen when the sun breaks through.
And just when you are thinking you are on the floor,
That is the moment fate will come knocking at your door.
Something's bound to happen though the leaves are brown,
Something's bound to happen though the rain falls down.
And just when you are thinking you are near the end,
That is the moment you will discover you've a friend.
Some days you are in a maze,
Never know which way to go.
You'll learn to find the proper turn,
Tears will turn to laughter,
You'll live happy ever after.

Something's bound to happen if you wait and see,
Something's bound to happen if you feel like me.
And just as you are thinking you are really through,
That is the moment somebody whispers, 'I love you'.

(Exeunt DICK and TOMMY U.R.)

CAPTAIN      (off L.)     Two points starboard!

MATE      (off L.)     Two points starboard.

CAPTAIN      (off)     Steady as she goes and heave! Heave! Heave!

(MUSIC 14 The MATE enters U.L. pulling on a rope over his shoulder.)

MATE      (as he enters)     Hard-a-port!

(The CAPTAIN enters standing on a little trolley pulled on by the MATE's rope. On front of trolley

1 - 1 - 14

is a ship's wheel; attached to back and resting on trolley is a prop anchor. CAPTAIN and MATE have cutlasses in their belts.)

(Moving D.R.) Hard-a-port.

CAPTAIN: Drop anchor!

MATE: (stops D.R., continuing to pull on rope and feeding it offstage) What?

CAPTAIN: Drop anchor!

MATE: I can't.

CAPTAIN: Why not?

MATE: I haven't got one.

(Trolley is now very close to MATE and he pulls it from under CAPTAIN's feet, toppling him off.)

CAPTAIN: Now look what you've done. (Rises and sets trolley upright and facing off R.) Well, where is the anchor? What have you done with it? (Discovers anchor.) Oh.

MATE: You see, you had it all the time.

CAPTAIN: Well, now we've found it, don't just stand there looking at it. Pick it up and drop it.

MATE: Pick it up and drop it?

CAPTAIN: Yes, pick it up and drop it.

MATE: (shrugs) Pick it up and drop it. (Picks up anchor and drops it on CAPTAIN's foot.)

CAPTAIN: OW! Not like that. Like this. (Picks up anchor and flings it at Audience. It returns as it is held by a rubber line.) Hm, doesn't seem to be holding. Well, we'll just have to hope the sea doesn't run downhill here. Now, we've got to find – (The trolley starts to be pulled off R.)

MATE: Ooh, look – it's moving all by itself.

CAPTAIN: It's drifting! Quick! After it!

(Trolley disappears off R. MATE runs off.)

Grab the anchor!

| | |
|---|---|
| MATE | (off) All right. (Re-enters with anchor unattached.) Here you are, here's the anchor. |
| CAPTAIN | You idiot! I didn't want just the anchor, I wanted the boat as well. |
| MATE | Oh. Well, what shall I do with it, then? |
| CAPTAIN | Oh, just drop it somewhere. |
| | (MATE drops it on CAPTAIN's toe.) |
| | OW! Don't keep dropping it on my toes. |
| MATE | (picking it up) Where else can I drop it? |
| CAPTAIN | Try your own toes for a change. |
| MATE | All right. (Drops it on own foot.) Oo! I don't like it. It tickles. |
| CAPTAIN | (throwing anchor off L. in disgust) Tickles! Ah, here's the bloke we want, Alderman Fitzwarren. |
| | (CAPTAIN bangs a tattoo on door - nothing happens. He shrugs and pulls bell-pull, it comes off in his hand and he throws it off D.L. in disgust. Enter JACK D.L. below shop door, holding a flower and pulling the petals off, and carrying bell-pull.) |
| JACK | She loves me, she loves me not - hullo, were you knocking? |
| CAPTAIN | Yes. |
| JACK | I thought so. Try the bell-pull. (Gives it to CAPTAIN and crosses C.) She loves me, she loves me not. |
| | (CAPTAIN is unable to think what to do with it, so replaces it in its socket. EFFECT 5. Bell jangles off. CAPTAIN and MATE exchange astonished looks.) |
| CAPTAIN | We thought you were all asleep. |
| | (JACK falls asleep. Audience shouts. JACK wakes.) |
| JACK | Thank you. She loves me, she loves me not. |
| CAPTAIN | Excuse us, if we're interrupting your horticultural |

|          | |
|----------|--|
|          | studies, but would you ask Alderman Fitzwarren if he could see us? We'd like to interest him in commissioning our ship, the 'Saucy Sal', for a trading voyage. |
| JACK     | Oh, well he's not in at the moment. She loves me – (Last petal.) she loves me not. Oh blow! There must be some way I can make Alice love me. (To them.) I say, how can I make a girl fall in love with me? |
| CAPTAIN  | (looks at him pointedly) Well, in your case it might be a bit difficult. Maybe you could rescue her from highwaymen or footpads or something. |
| JACK     | But I don't know any footpads or highwaymen. |
| CAPTAIN  | Oh, you don't need real ones – just get some blokes to pretend they are. |
| JACK     | That's a jolly good idea, and it's very nice of you to offer to do it. |
| CAPTAIN  | Eh? What?   ⎫ (Together.) |
| MATE     | Us?         ⎭ |
| MATE     | But we might get hurt. |
| JACK     | Not with me doing the rescuing. And I tell you what, I'll put in a good word for you with old Fitzwarren. But we'd better practise it a bit first. I know, I'll tell Sarah, our cook, it's time to get her beer, and you can pretend to be footpads and waylay her as she comes out. Now stand by while I get her. (Exit into shop.) |
| CAPTAIN  | Now look what you've done. |
| MATE     | Me? |
| CAPTAIN  | Yes, you – suggesting all those silly ideas. Well, I suppose we'll have to go through with it. (Crouches beside shop door.) You get behind me.<br><br>(MATE gets behind him – as far U.S. as he can.)<br><br>(Turns.) Not all that far behind me. |
| MATE     | Oh. (Comes D.S.) |

| | |
|---|---|
| CAPTAIN | In fact, I think it would be better if I got behind you. (Does so.) |
| MATE | I don't. (Gets behind CAPTAIN.) |
| CAPTAIN | Well, I do. (Gets behind MATE.) |
| | (They continue trying to hide behind each other as SARAH enters from shop, carrying a jug and humming happily to herself as she crosses to inn and exits. JACK runs on.) |
| JACK | Stop! Unhand that - haven't you done it yet? |
| CAPTAIN | There, we've missed her. (To MATE.) Your fault again. |
| MATE | My fault? |
| CAPTAIN | Yes, you shouldn't be so nervous. |
| JACK | Well, stand by to catch her on the way back. |
| | (JACK exits into shop. CAPTAIN and MATE line up side by side at inn door. Enter SARAH with jug above inn piece, still humming happily. She passes them, registers that they are there, turns back and lines up beside them.) |
| SARAH | Hullo, what are you doing? |
| CAPTAIN and MATE | (in hoarse whispers) We're waiting. |
| SARAH | (imitating whisper) What for? |
| CAPTAIN | (whispering) Some old bag who just went in to get a jug of beer. |
| SARAH | Some old bag! |
| MATE | (whispering) Yes, when the old witch comes out we're going to pounce on her and demand her money or her life. |
| SARAH | Oh, are you? We'll see about that. Old witch, indeed. Just keep an eye on my beer, will you? (Puts jug down in C.) I'll be back in a minute. |
| CAP and MATE | All right. |
| | (Exit SARAH above inn. Slight pause.) |

| | |
|---|---|
| MATE | (whispering)   I say, she's a long time, isn't she? |
| CAPTAIN | (whispering)   Ssh, I think she's coming. |
| | (Enter SARAH through inn door.  CAPTAIN draws his cutlass and the handle comes away in his hand.) |
| | Stand and deliver!  Your money or your life! (Sees handle.)   Oh. |
| MATE | Here, have mine.   (Draws his and only gets handle.)   Oh. |
| SARAH | Try these instead.   (Produces two syphons from behind her back and squirts CAPTAIN and MATE.) |
| CAP and MATE | Oooo!   (They fall down.) |
| SARAH | Two-syphon Sarah, they call me.   (Puts syphons back in pub.) |
| | (JACK rushes on from shop.) |
| JACK | Stop!  Unhand that woman!  Oh.  Don't you want to be rescued? |
| SARAH | No, thank you.   (Picks up beer jug and exits into shop.) |
| JACK | Oh.   (Crosses to CAPTAIN and MATE.)   I say, did something go wrong? |
| | (CAPTAIN and MATE rise.) |
| CAPTAIN | Yes, it did.  We were the ones that needed rescuing, not her. |
| JACK | Never mind, I expect you'll do it better next time. |
| CAPTAIN | Next time? |
| MATE | Next time? |
| CAPTAIN | You don't think we're going to go through that again, do you? |
| JACK | Of course.  That was only a try-out.  Besides, if you don't, I shan't use my influence with old Fitzwarren for you. |
| ALICE | (off, in shop)   Jack!  Jack! |
| JACK | There!  She's coming!  Quick, take up your places. |

|  |  |
|---|---|
|  | I'll hide here. |
|  | (JACK runs off D.L. CAPTAIN and MATE press themselves to the wall on either side of the shop door, CAPTAIN on R. and MATE on L.) |
| ALICE | (appearing in doorway) Jack! |
| CAPTAIN | Pounce! |
|  | (CAPTAIN and MATE pounce just as ALICE has turned to go back and grab each other.) |
| CAP and MATE | Got her! |
| ALICE | Is anything the matter? |
|  | (They look up, realise their mistake and release each other.) |
| CAPTAIN | Quick! Grab her! |
|  | (They grasp an arm each and drag ALICE to C.) |
| ALICE | Help! Help! Thieves! Help! ⎫ |
| CAP and MATE | Your money or your life! ⎬ (Together.) |
|  | (TOMMY enters U.R., sees the struggle and beckons frantically to R.) |
| TOMMY | MEOW! |
|  | (At the same time enter JACK D.L.) |
| JACK | Stop! Unhand that – |
|  | (Trips over TOMMY and falls as DICK enters U.R.) |
| DICK | What's wrong, Tommy? Thieves, eh? (Advancing on CAPTAIN.) Let go, you ruffian, take that! (DICK knocks the CAPTAIN aside.) |
| CAPTAIN | OW! |
| DICK | And you, take that! (Deals similarly with MATE.) |
| MATE | OW! |
|  | (TOMMY bites CAPTAIN in the seat of his pants.) |
| CAPTAIN | Ouch! Help! A tiger! |
|  | (TOMMY bites MATE in the seat of his pants.) |

| | |
|---|---|
| MATE | Ouch! I've been bitten by a lion! |
| JACK | (rising)   Hey, wait a minute, I'm doing the rescuing - |
| DICK | What, another of them!   (DICK sends JACK flying.) |
| JACK | OW! |
| | (TOMMY bites him in the seat of his pants.) |
| | Ouch! A panther's bitten me! |
| | (TOMMY chases CAPTAIN, MATE and JACK off L.) |
| DICK | That's dealt with them. I hope they didn't harm you. |
| ALICE | No, I'm quite all right, thanks to you. |
| DICK | Then I'm almost grateful to them for giving me the chance to rescue such a pretty girl. Tell me, what is your name? |
| ALICE | Alice - Alice Fitzwarren. |
| DICK | And mine's Dick Whittington. |
| ALICE | I'm sure my father will want to reward you, Master Whittington. Where can he find you? |
| DICK | Oh, please, I need no reward. And as to where to find me - well, I've only just arrived in London so before I find somewhere to live I must find somewhere to work. |
| ALICE | But that's splendid. My father owns this shop. I told him this morning he needed a new apprentice, so now I'll tell him I've found one. That is, if you'd like to be his apprentice. |
| DICK | I'd like to be anything that keeps me near you. There's only one thing - Tommy, my cat, would have to come with me. |
| ALICE | Oh, that's all right. Father loves cats. Well, I've never heard him say he doesn't. |
| DICK | As a matter of fact, he hasn't been my cat long, but the funny thing is, I met him just where we're standing now, in front of this pump. It seems all my pleasantest meetings take place here. |

(MUSIC 15  'YOU'RE SO LOVELY')

She's so lovely - indescribable -
Her eyes are like the morning mist when April's on its way.

ALICE
He's so handsome, brave and lovable
His voice is low and gentle like the breaking of the day.

DICK
How could I deserve a love so fine?

ALICE
I would give my soul to make you mine,

BOTH
Then forever I would cherish him/her,
And keep him/her ever happy/lovely till the day I die.

(Enter FITZWARREN U. L. with TOMMY.)

FITZWARREN
Good dog, good dog, I'll give you a biscuit when I get home.

TOMMY
(slightly outraged)    Meow!

FITZWARREN
I beg your pardon!

TOMMY
MEOW!

FITZWARREN
Hm, curious sounding dog.    (To ALICE.)
Excuse me, madam, is this your dog?    (Peers at her.)    Oh, pardon me, haven't we met somewhere before?

ALICE
Father - I'm your daughter, Alice.

FITZWARREN
(shaking hands with her)    Ah, then we have met before.

ALICE
And it isn't a dog. It's a cat.

DICK
Yes, it's my cat, Tommy.

ALICE
(stroking TOMMY)    Hullo, Tommy. Oh, you're very beautiful, aren't you?

TOMMY
(agrees)

ALICE
This is somebody you haven't met before, Father.
Dick Whittington, your new apprentice.

FITZWARREN
Oh, splendid, how do you -  My new what, did you say?

| | |
|---|---|
| ALICE | Your new apprentice. I've just engaged him for you. |
| FITZWARREN | But - but - I only said I'd think about it. I mean, apprentices cost money. Do you realise I already pay Jack a shilling a week? |
| ALICE | In that case, we'd better make it a shilling for Dick as well. |
| FITZWARREN | What! Do you want to ruin me? |
| ALICE | Well, it's not very much to pay somebody who's just saved my life. |
| FITZWARREN | Eh? |
| ALICE | I was attacked by thieves and Dick saved me. |
| TOMMY | (taps her with a paw and points to himself) |
| ALICE | Oh, and Tommy, too, of course. |
| FITZWARREN | My child, why didn't you tell me before?  (To TOMMY.)  My dear boy, (To DICK.) my dear dog - er - cat, what can I do to show my gratitude? |
| ALICE | Make Dick your apprentice at a shilling a week. |
| FITZWARREN | I've just had a splendid idea. I'll make you my apprentice at a shilling a week. No, let's not be niggardly. At one shilling and <u>threepence</u> a week. |
| DICK | Thank you very much, Mr Fitzwarren. Isn't that splendid, Tommy? |
| TOMMY | (agrees) |
| | (CHORUS enter L. and R., chattering excitedly. Enter SARAH from shop, putting on a Beauty Queen-type ribbon over one shoulder.) |
| FITZWARREN | Hullo, where's everybody off to? |
| SARAH | The Lord Mayor's Show, of course. The Butchers' Guild have asked me to be their Miss Steak this year. |
| FITZWARREN | I'm not surprised. |
| ALICE | Oh. |

(SARAH turns and shows wording on back of ribbon 'MISS STEAK, 1401'.)

You must hurry, too, Father. You're supposed to lead the Lord Mayor's procession.

FITZWARREN  Am I?

ALICE  Well, you always do every year.

FITZWARREN  Oh yes, so I do. I remember last year we ended up in the river - I can't think why.   (Almost walks off front of stage.)

SARAH  (just pulling him back in time)   Aah!

FITZWARREN  Yes, maybe you're right, the other way's quicker. Come on then - to the Lord Mayor's Show.

(MUSIC 16   'THE LORD MAYOR'S SHOW')

ALL
We're going to the Lord Mayor's Show -
   Today's a great holiday.
The silver lining
Of the clouds is shining,
   All the world is happy and gay.

We're going to the Lord Mayor's Show -
   The town is taking the air.
We'll put something fresh on
For the grand procession,
   And we'll find the fun of the fair.

The lads and lasses
Of all the classes,
In droves and masses,
   We swear,
Are enigmatically,
Coat and hatically,
Most emphatically,
   THERE!

The sun's above, the world's in love,
   Our hearts with hope are aglow.
Strike up the band!
And dancing hand in hand,
   We're off to see the Lord Mayor's Show!

(BLACKOUT. Close traverse tabs. Fly in Scene 2 Frontcloth, if used.)

## PART I

### Scene Two - PETTICOAT LANE

(Front cloth, a street scene, or tabs. If cloth is used, tabs to begin.
MUSIC 17.    GREEN FLASH L., and GREEN SPOT up as KING RAT
enters L.)

KING RAT        Confusion take that irksome fay!
                Her ward doth prosper day by day;
                By all he's held in high esteem,
                And even blest with love's young dream.
                But dreams to nightmares swift can turn
                As Master Whittington shall learn.
                His sweet success in love doth wrack
                The jealous heart of Idle Jack,
                And I'll this spark of envy use
                To light a highly potent fuse.
                But soft - for Idle Jack draws near,
                I'll wait unseen his thoughts to hear.

                (He exits L. Traverse tabs open. LIGHTS UP.
                Enter JACK R., with flower, pulling the petals off.)

JACK            She loves me, she loves me not, she loves me -
                (Last petal.)   she loves me not. It's no use,
                nobody seems to grow flowers with the right
                number of petals. Not that I stand much chance
                since that Dick Whittington pinched my rescue.
                And he's no good as an apprentice - he will work so
                hard. It just makes me want to go to sleep.
                (He falls asleep. Audience shout. He wakes.)
                Oh, thank you.

CAPTAIN         (off L.)    Wilfrid! Wilfrid!

JACK            Oh dear, here comes one of those sailors. They're
                always on at me to use my influence with
                Fitzwarren for them. I'll sneak away before he
                sees me.    (Tip-toes towards R.)

MATE            (off R.)    Captain Cuttle! Captain Cuttle!

JACK            (dithering to and fro)    Oo, I'm caught.

                (Enter CAPTAIN backwards L.)

CAPTAIN         Wilfrid! Wilfrid Scuttle! Oh, where have you got

|  |  |
|---|---|
|  | to, Wilfrid? |
|  | (Enter MATE backwards R.) |
| MATE | Captain Cuttle! Where are you, Captain? |
| CAPTAIN | (stopping just short of JACK) I'm here. Where are you? |
| MATE | (stopping just short of JACK on other side) I'm here too. |
|  | (JACK holds himself in with his arms pressed close to his sides.) |
| CAPTAIN | Well, I can't see you. |
| MATE | I can't see you, neither. |
| CAPTAIN | We'd better look for each other somewhere else, then. |
|  | (They move forward to L. and R. to JACK's relief, but then circle round U.S. and walk towards him, with their heads averted looking for each other until they collide with him in C. and turn and see him.) |
| CAPTAIN and MATE | Idle Jack! (They grab him and as they do so, see each other.) Hullo, fancy meeting you here. (They shake hands heartily and exchange pleasantries.) |
| JACK | Well, now you've met again, I expect you'll have a lot to say to each other, so I'll leave you alone. |
|  | (He tries to get away, but they yank him back by his collar.) |
| CAPTAIN | Oh no, you don't. We've been looking for you. When are you going to fix up that commission for us with Fitzwarren, like you promised? I'm beginning to think you haven't as much influence with him as you made out. |
| JACK | What? Why, Fitzy and I are just like that. (Indicates by pressing two fingers together.) I'll speak to him about it the very next time I see him. |
| FITZWARREN | (off R.) Idle Jack! Idle Jack! (He enters.) |

| | |
|---|---|
| JACK | Oh dear. |
| FITZWARREN | (bumps into JACK) Sorry. |
| JACK | Not at all. (Starts to sneak off R.) |
| FITZWARREN | (does a double take and pulls him back) Ah, it's you, you lazy, good-for-nothing scoundrel. |
| CAPTAIN | (pressing two fingers together) Just like that, eh? |
| FITZWARREN | (pulling him to R.) Come along at once, Jack. Don't waste your time with these idle rascals. They'll do you no good. |
| | (CAPTAIN and MATE pull JACK L.) |
| CAPTAIN | They certainly won't, if you don't do us some. |
| FITZWARREN | (pulling JACK R.) They're just a pair of wastrels. Drunkards, too, I expect. |
| | (CAPTAIN and MATE pull JACK L.) |
| CAPTAIN | Start using that influence. |
| | (The tug-o-war continues.) |
| JACK | I'm trying to. Oh dear, I wish I could think of a way out of this. |
| | (GREEN FLASH L. <u>MUSIC 18</u> and KING RAT enters. CAPTAIN and MATE see him, just as FITZWARREN is pulling JACK to R. They faint, leaving JACK and FITZWARREN to fall over.) |
| FITZWARREN | There, I said so. They're drunk. (Rises and crosses to KING RAT.) And I suppose this is another of your disreputable companions. (Peers at KING RAT.) Yes, I thought as much. (Double takes on him.) Aah! (Rushes off R., yelling.) |
| | (JACK rises and KING RAT moves in beside him.) |
| JACK | What's the matter with everybody suddenly? |
| KING RAT | Hist! |
| | (JACK turns and falls back in fright.) |
| | Nay, Idle Jack, be not afraid, |

|           | For I have come to give ye aid. |
|-----------|---|
| JACK      | (scrabbling at the ground with his feet trying to get up)<br>I'd rather go, if you don't mind,<br>If only I my feet could find. |
| KING RAT  | Why, here they are.    (He drags JACK to his feet.) |
| JACK      | Ow! Someone, help! |
| KING RAT  | Hush, prithee, there's no need to yelp.<br>Would'st o'er thy rival win the day?<br>Then list, I'll tell ye how ye may.<br>Tomorrow, as I think ye know,<br>Thy master to his bank will go<br>And gather certain monies there,<br>Which in his safe he'll place with care.<br>This done, 'tis time for ye to act.<br>Ye must the gold therein extract.<br>And slyly place it - where d'ye think? |
| JACK      | Well, nowhere, or I'll land in clink. |
| KING RAT  | Fool! Place it in thy rival's purse;<br>And when Fitzwarren starts to curse,<br>Denounce young Whittington at once.<br>Dost understand? |
| JACK      | No. |
| KING RAT  | Th'art a dunce!<br>Think! When on him they find the loot - |
| JACK      | I've got it! They'll give him the boot! |
| KING RAT  | Aye, 'twill disgrace him in all eyes.<br>Your Alice will her thoughts revise,<br>And surely give her heart to you. |
| JACK      | You think she will? |
| KING RAT  | I'm certain. |
| JACK      | Coo!<br>Well then, I'll do it. |
| KING RAT  | Ah, good man!<br>I'll leave ye to digest the plan, |

|   |   |
|---|---|
| | And if aught further help ye need, |
| | King Rat will join thee with all speed. |
| JACK | Thanks, Ratty. |
| KING RAT | Farewell! |
| JACK | Must you dash? |
| KING RAT | (bowing)    For now. |
| | (GREEN FLASH as he exits L.) |
| JACK | Nice bloke, but rather flash. Still, he had some very good ideas. The only thing is, how am I going to break open the safe? (Moves forward and trips over the inert SAILORS.) Oops. I know, I'll get these two to help me. (Shaking them.)    Oi! Wake up! Come on, wakey, wakey, show a toe. |
| | (CAPTAIN and MATE recover and sit up.) |
| CAPTAIN | Oo, has old grim and grisly gone? |
| MATE | 'Cos if he hasn't I'm going to faint again. |
| JACK | Old Ratty? Yes, he's gone.    (Helps them to rise.) |
| MATE | Good, then let's go before he comes back. |
| JACK | Wait a minute, I want your help. |
| CAP and MATE | (moving L.)    Well, you can't have it. |
| JACK | I'll have to call old Ratty back then. |
| CAP and MATE | (returning)    What do you want us to do? |
| JACK | Oh, just help me break open a safe and steal some money. |
| MATE | But that's naughty. |
| JACK | Not really, you see we don't steal the money for ourselves, we plant it on that Dick Whittington bloke, and then you two say you saw him take it. |
| MATE | But that's fibbing. |
| JACK | Yes, but Fitzy will be so grateful to you he'll commission your ship. Now, will you do it? |

| | |
|---|---|
| CAP and MATE | No.    (They move away.) |
| JACK | (calling)    Oh, Ratty! |
| CAP and MATE | (returning)    Yes. |
| CAPTAIN | (looks suspiciously round on all sides)    When do we do the dirty deed? |
| JACK | Tomorrow. |
| CAPTAIN | Tomorrow? |
| MATE | Tomorrow? |
| JACK | Tomorrow. |
| ALL | Tomorrow!  Ssh! |
| | (<u>MUSIC 19</u>   'DIRTY WORK'    (Close traverse tabs slowly during number.  Fly out cloth.) |
| | If there's dirty work to do without the slightest fuss, <br> Call us on the telephone and leave the rest to us. <br> If you've got a money-box that you would like to rob, <br> Our fees are very reasonable - a bob a job. |
| CAPTAIN | If you know a man to whom you'd like to give a fright, <br> We pull awful faces in the middle of the night. <br> If you have an enemy you'd really like to fix, <br> We cut his braces very neatly - |
| ALL | For one and six. |
| JACK | If there's lots of nasty people you would like to do, <br> We pack them off to Dover <br> (Or wherever is locally suitable, that scans.) <br>                                                               on the seven twenty-two. <br> If there should be a motorist who nearly knocks you down, <br> We syphon all his petrol out - |
| ALL | For half-a-crown. |
| MATE | We've got knuckle-dusters and a special kind of cosh; <br> We wear leather jackets and we call each other 'Tosh'. <br> If you've done a something what you hadn't oughter did, |

We hush it all up very nice -

ALL                                                  For half a quid.

If there's dirty work to do without a lot of fuss,
Call us on the telephone and leave the rest to us.
We are not contending for the plaudits of the mob,
We merely hope you'll pay our wages - a bob a job.

(As they begin to exit -

BLACKOUT

Open traverse tabs.)

PART I

Scene Three - FITZWARREN'S STORES

(Full set. Backing of flats, set in front of rostrum, with door C. with shop bell attached. Door hinged on R., opening on stage. Door knob on L. String of onions hanging to R. of door, tailor's dummy set R. of door. Shop wing L., with high shelf with jar of lollipops on it. Shop wing R., with clock face painted on it and movable hands. R.C. a cash desk on which is a large cash register with practical drawer, FITZ-WARREN's bowler hat and a prop banana. Under desk, a large safe in which is a bottle of Guinness. L.C. a counter running up and down stage. On counter a movable cheese, side of bacon, string of sausages, pad of paper and pencil, telephone and a pair of scissors. Set of kitchen steps behind counter.

SARAH is discovered cleaning the shop with broom and dustpan and brush. Music has continued from Scene 2.)

(MUSIC 20 'DIRTY WORK')

SARAH
When there's dirty work to do I do it with a will,
In fact I work so very hard it nearly makes me ill.
I always work to music, either classical or pop,
Which helps me do the dirty work in - the bloomin' shop.

Dust and clean and brush and mop and brush and clean and dust;
Get the whole place done before it's op'ning time or bust.
Ev'rything looks tidy now, and so I'd better stop
And put the cleaning things away and - then open shop.

Whew! There now, the shop's ready for the day. (Sees some dust on the floor.) Oh no, missed a bit.

(Bends to brush it up with behind pointing to R. FITZWARREN enters D.R. and bumps into her.)

FITZWARREN   Oops!   (Peers at her behind.)   What's this?

SARAH   Eh?

FITZWARREN   (patting her)   Oh, so sorry, Tommy.

| | |
|---|---|
| SARAH | (on her dignity) Tommy? How dare you call me a cat. (EFFECT 6. Telephone bell rings.) I'll get it. (Picks up receiver.) Hello, Fitzwarren's Stores. Yes, one minute, please. (Holding out receiver.) It's for you. |
| FITZWARREN | (picks up banana) Hullo, Fitzwarren speaking. |
| SARAH | Put that banana down, Fitzy. The telephone's over here. |
| FITZWARREN | (puts banana down) Oh. (Shouting.) Hullo, Fitzwarren speaking. (Normal voice.) I can't hear them. |
| SARAH | (takes receiver towards him as far as cord will go) That's as far as it will go. Try again. |
| FITZWARREN | (shouting) Hullo, Fitzwarren speaking. (Normal voice.) I still can't hear them. |
| SARAH | (shouting into phone) He says he can't hear you. Oh! (Hastily moves receiver away, then listens again.) They say they can't hear you either. |
| FITZWARREN | Well, I can't shout any louder. Tell them to get a bigger 'phone. |
| SARAH | No, I've got it. (Takes scissors from counter, cuts cord and takes receiver over to FITZWARREN.) There you are. |
| FITZWARREN | That's better. (Into 'phone.) Hullo? |
| SARAH | Hullo. |
| FITZWARREN | Hullo? |
| SARAH | Hullo. |
| FITZWARREN | Who's that? |
| SARAH | Me. |
| FITZWARREN | Where are you? |
| SARAH | Here. |
| BOTH | (turning and shaking hands) Hul-lo! |
| FITZWARREN | (pulling his hand away) Tcha! |

(SARAH breaks L., chuckling.)

There's something wrong with this 'phone. (Holds up end of cord.) I think we've been cut off. (Throws receiver off R. and picks up bowler.) Look after the shop while I'm out, Sarah.

SARAH   Who, me? But what about me cooking? I can't sweat over a hot stove and serve over a shop counter at one and the same time, can I?

FITZWARREN   I'm afraid you'll have to. Dick's helping Alice to clear out the storeroom, Jack's late as usual and I've got to get the money for the wages. (Moves up and bumps into dummy.) Quick, bring some water, somebody's fainted!

SARAH   It's the dummy.

FITZWARREN   (peering at it) Oh yes. (Sets it upright.) There should be some new ones arriving today. (Gropes for door.) Where's the door got to? (Grasps one of the onions on string.) Ah, here's the knob. (Discovers other onions.) Good gracious, it's had babies. I wonder which is the right one?

SARAH   (leading him to door) Try this one.

FITZWARREN   Ah, yes, thank you. Ta-ta for now. (Exit.)

SARAH   Well, I'd better get back to me kitchen or I'll never get me cooking done, but I bet that shop bell starts ringing the minute my back is turned.

(Exit L. Slight pause. A CHORUS GIRL enters - bell on door rings - and comes to counter. SARAH runs on L. to behind counter. To Audience.)

There, what did I tell you? (To CHORUS GIRL.) Good morning, madam, what can I get you? Any tea, coffee, sugar, cocoa, butter, lard, marge or marg this morning? Or cheese - We've got some beautiful cheese today. (Whistles. MUSIC whizz. Cheese moves down counter. Fishing line attached to cheese, running through hole in counter and operated by SARAH. SARAH sniffs.) Yes, it's really nice and ripe. (Moves cheese back again.) How about sausages? These are beauties. (Picks up string of sausages.) Caught only this morning, and it's just the season for them now there's an 'R' in the month. So good for exercise, too. (Skips with them.) And they can be worn off the shoulder like this - (Demonstrates.) or carelessly flung round the neck. (Hits CHORUS GIRL in face with them as she does so.) Oops, so sorry, madam. (Throws them aside and picks up bacon.) What about bacon? Delicious long back, home smoked - in fact, I smoke nothing else. (Uses bacon to hit imaginary fly on counter then flicks it off with finger.) Got it! Then there's tinned goods, or fish-paste, or jams, jellies, marmalade, flour, custard powder, candles, creams and polishes and - and - what can I get you?

CHORUS GIRL     I want a ha'penny lollipop.

SARAH           (stunned)     A ha'penny lollipop? A ha'p - (Overcomes her natural impulses.) Certainly, madam. (Looks round for them.) Lollipops, lollipops, lollipops. (Sees them on shelf.) Ah, lollipops. (Puts steps under shelf, climbs up, brings down jar, unscrews lid, takes out lollipop after getting hand stuck in jar and removing it with difficulty, smiling with murderous sweetness at CHORUS GIRL all the while. Then replaces lid, climbs up steps, puts jar back on shelf, comes down steps and hands lollipop, a green one, to CHORUS GIRL.) There we are, madam.

CHORUS GIRL     (looks at it dubiously)     I'd like a red one, please.

SARAH           (gulps)     A red one. Certainly. (Snatches back lollipop, flashes CHORUS GIRL a dazzlingly false smile, slams lollipop on counter, stamps up steps, turns to throw CHORUS GIRL another smile and almost over-balances, brings down jar, unscrews lid and gets hand stuck. Tugging violently to get it out.)     You did say a red one?

CHORUS GIRL    Yes, a red one.

SARAH    A red one.    (With a tremendous heave pulls a yellow one out.)    There we -    (Sees colour.) A red one?

CHORUS GIRL    A red one.

SARAH    A red one.    (Puts yellow lollipop on counter, plunges hand in jar again, grips jar between knees, tugs so hard she falls over and brings out a red lollipop with a bent stick.)    One bent red lollipop.    (Gives it to CHORUS GIRL, replaces lid, climbs steps, puts jar back and comes down. Discovers green and yellow lollipops on counter. Flies up steps, flies down with jar, puts in lollipops, rescrews lid, flies up steps to replace jar, flies down again and sighs with relief.)

CHORUS GIRL    (eating lollipop)    How much is it, please?

SARAH    How much. Er - one ha'penny lollipop. Well, at two for a penny, that's -    (Desperately calculates on fingers.)    Er - er - er - twos into one won't go - carry four - take away the number you first thought of - um.    (Scribbles hurriedly on pad, rapidly turning over pages till she finishes scribbling on counter.)    One ha'penny! Brilliant!

(CHORUS GIRL hands her a £5 note. SARAH is taken aback.)

Er - you haven't anything a little smaller?

CHORUS GIRL    No, they don't make five pound notes any smaller.

SARAH    Er - no, hm. I'll just get you your change, madam.    (Runs to cash desk, depresses key on cash register, and the drawer shoots out and knocks her over - catch holding drawer worked by SARAH. She rises, puts note in till, takes out a lot of change, shuts drawer and runs back to counter. Counts this into CHORUS GIRL's hand.) Now, that's one penny, two, three, fivepence, ten, twenty, thirty, forty, fifty and fifty's a pound, and two, three, four, five pounds.

| | | |
|---|---|---|
| CHORUS GIRL | | Thank you.   (Counts through change very carefully.) |
| SARAH | | No, madam, thank you. |
| CHORUS GIRL | | It's a ha'penny short. |
| SARAH | | What?   (Examines change.)   Blimey, so it is. I'm so sorry, madam. I'll get your ha'penny straight away.   (SARAH runs back to cash desk and is about to depress key, but remembers, so jumps aside and pulls a face at the drawer, then depresses key. Drawer does not open. She depresses key again, it still does not open. She moves in to see what is wrong. Drawer flies out and knocks her over. She rises with shrug, takes halfpenny from till, runs to counter, and gives it to CHORUS GIRL, who has just finished her lollipop.)   Your ha'penny, madam. |
| CHORUS GIRL | | Thank you.   (Puts it in pocket and takes out another £5 note.)   I'd like another lollipop, please. |
| SARAH | | What!   (Runs up steps, grabs jar from the shelf and runs down again.)   Here, never mind about the money, I'll give you one, in fact you can have the bloomin' lot. There you are.   (Presses jar on CHORUS GIRL and hustles her to door.)   Thank you so much. Good day, madam, good day.   (Pushes her out and leans, panting, on the door.)   And I hope they make her sick. Oh, what a nasty thing to say.   (Grabs large packet labelled 'BICARB' from counter and throws it after CHORUS GIRL.)   Oi! There's some tummy-ache powder to go with 'em.   (Moves down.)   Now if that bell goes again I'll - I'll - well, I suppose I'll answer it.   (Exit D.L.) |

(Slight pause. Enter TOMMY through door, bell rings. He leaves door open and moves in front of counter. SARAH rushes back.)

Go away! We haven't got any lollipops. We've sold out! We've - there, I'm suffering from hallelujah-kinations now.   (Exit D.L.)

| | |
|---|---|
| TOMMY | (looks after her with head on one side, then runs up and shuts door with behind to make bell ring and hurries to hide U. S. of counter) |
| SARAH | (rushing on) Now what is - (Strums on counter with fingers.) Well, I'm sure I heard the bell that time. I must be going bonkers. (Moves C. To Audience.) I say, will you help me? Did you hear that bell ring just then? |
| TOMMY | (comes out of hiding, keeping behind SARAH and shakes head vigorously to indicate to Audience to say 'No') |
| SARAH | No, don't muck about. Did you or didn't you? - I don't know, some of you say 'Yes' and some of you say 'No', there's no a-trusting of you. I know, I'll ask this lot down here. (To ORCHESTRA.) Boys, did you hear that bell ring? |
| ORCHESTRA | NO! |
| SARAH | Ah, now I know somebody rang it. I wonder where they're hiding? |
| | (Moves to look round cash desk with TOMMY trotting behind her. To Audience.) |
| | Are they over here? - No. Well, are they over here? |
| | (Moves to look behind U. S. end of counter, TOMMY following.) |
| | No. Well, round here then? (Moves behind counter.) Ah, I know. |
| | (Drops down on all fours behind counter and starts to creep round. TOMMY is puzzled as to where she has got to and creeps down his side of counter. They meet nose to nose below counter, startling each other and jumping back.) |
| | Oh, Tommy, it was you all the time. (Rises.) You naughty cat, you. |
| TOMMY | (rolls on his back, waving his paws in the air) |
| SARAH | No, it's no use trying your wiles on me. I'm very annoyed with you. |

| | |
|---|---|
| TOMMY | (rises, looking at her appealingly, head on one side)   Meow! |
| SARAH | Oh yes, I know what you're thinking. You're thinking you can wheedle me into giving you a saucer of milk, aren't you? |
| TOMMY | (nods and purrs) |
| SARAH | Yes, well I'm not going to. |
| TOMMY | (purrs harder, rubbing himself against her legs) |
| SARAH | No, you won't get round me. |
| TOMMY | (moves round purring and rubs against L. side of legs) |
| SARAH | Oh, you have, haven't you? Well, come on then, you soppy thing. I've got a nice bit of fish you can have, too. |
| | (TOMMY, very pleased with himself, scampers off L. and she follows. Slight pause. FITZWARREN enters through door, carrying money-bag.) |
| FITZWARREN | Here we are, the money for the wages. (Crosses to safe.) |
| | (CAPTAIN, MATE and JACK's faces appear round door.) |
| JACK, CAPTAIN and MATE | Ah! |
| FITZWARREN | Hm, sounds as if there's a wind getting up. |
| | (Starts to put money in safe, and JACK, carrying a tool bag and DICK's purse, CAPTAIN and MATE creep in behind him.) |
| | It's funny, but ever since I left the bank I've been followed. |
| | (Others look at each other in consternation for a moment, then run to beside dummy and assume static postures.) |
| | There, now I must go and do me accounts. (Moves up to shut door.)   Ah, the new |

|  |  |
|---|---|
|  | dummies have arrived. (Eyes them with head on one side.) Hm, not very lifelike. (Exit U.R.) |
| JACK | (in dramatic whisper) Now's our chance, but we must be quiet. |
|  | (MATE clears his throat nervously and loudly.) |
|  | (Turns, severely putting finger to lips.) Ssh! |
| CAPTAIN | (does likewise) <u>Ssh!</u> |
| MATE | (looks abashed, then turns and puts his finger to lips at dummy) SSH! |
| JACK | (passing them to CAPTAIN) Here, take the tools. |
| CAPTAIN | Here, take the tools. (He passes them to MATE.) |
| MATE | Here, take the tools. (Passes them to nothing and they drop with a clatter.) |
| JACK and CAPTAIN | (bellowing) QUIET! (They tip-toe elaborately down to safe.) |
| JACK | (dramatically) Right - we're there! Now all we have to do is open the safe and put the money in Dick's purse here. Let's have the tools. |
|  | (MATE throws bag at JACK's feet.) |
|  | OW! (Hops round holding foot.) |
| CAPTAIN | (to MATE) SSH! |
| MATE | What are you shushing me for? He's making all the noise. |
| CAPTAIN | So he is. |
| CAP and MATE | (to JACK) SSSSSSSSSSHHHHHHHHH! |
| JACK | Look out! You're drenching me! Let's get on and open the safe, but quietly. (Brings out prop road drill from bag.) |
| CAPTAIN | Won't that be a bit noisy? |
| JACK | No, it's fitted with a silencer. (Holds it against safe, <u>EFFECT 7</u>. Tremendous noise of |

1 - 3 - 39

|  |  |
|---|---|
|  | road drill.  JACK vibrates exaggeratedly.) |
|  | (MATE kneels down to put hammers and chisels into bag.) |
|  | (Shouting.)    You see, doesn't make any noise at all. |
| CAPTAIN | (coming to R. of safe.  Shouting)    Is it getting anywhere? |
| JACK | (shouting)    No. |
|  | (Drill slips off safe onto CAPTAIN's toe.) |
| CAPTAIN | OW! |
| JACK | Sorry. |
|  | (With an effort, JACK lifts drill from CAPTAIN's toe and turning to L., accidentally places it on the MATE's behind.  MATE leaps up clutching himself.) |
| MATE | WAAH!    (Runs off L.) |
| CAPTAIN | Switch it off! |
| JACK | I'm trying to! |
|  | (Drill noise stops.) |
|  | Ah.    (Puts drill down, but continues to vibrate.) There's nothing else for it, we'll have to use the dynamite.    (Takes dynamite – stick of rock – to which is attached a length of fuse, from bag.) |
| CAPTAIN | D-d-dynamite? |
| JACK | Yes, but you'd better take it.  My hands are still shaking and I might drop it. |
|  | (CAPTAIN unwillingly takes it.) |
|  | If you drop it, it explodes. |
| CAPTAIN | (almost drops it, but catches it before it reaches floor)    I d-don't want it. |
|  | (Enter MATE L., rubbing his behind.) |
|  | Here, you have this. |
|  | (Throws it to MATE, who catches it.) |

| | |
|---|---|
| MATE | Thank you.    (Bites a piece from it.)    Um, tastes good.   What is it? |
| CAPTAIN | Dynamite. |
| MATE | Dynamite, eh?    (Takes another bite, then the penny drops.)    AAH!    (Lets go of it and catches it again, then stands with knees trembling, knocks from ORCHESTRA.) |
| JACK | (has recovered from his vibrations)    Don't muck about with it.  We're going to set it off.  Put it down in front of the safe. |
| | (MATE does so very gingerly while JACK takes a large box of matches from bag.) |
| | Now I light the fuse.    (Pretends to do so. EFFECT 8.  Hissing noise off.)    Then we stroll to a safe distance. |
| | (They stroll L. a few paces, then break into a run.) |
| | And when the hissing stops, it'll go off. |
| | (Hissing continues for a second or two, then stops. They clamp their hands to their ears and there is a small pop (pop-gun) EFFECT 9.  They straighten up a little put out.) |
| CAPTAIN | I don't think it's worked properly. |
| | (SARAH heard off L. singing, 'Oh, what a beautiful morning'.) |
| MATE | Somebody's coming! |
| CAPTAIN | We must hide! |
| JACK | Gather up the stuff! |
| | (They quickly gather everything up and rush off behind wing R. as SARAH enters L. and crosses to safe, still singing.  Their heads come round wing to watch her as she looks at clock.) |
| SARAH | Oh, dear me no.    (Moves the hands on a bit, then opens safe and takes out a large bottle of Guinness.)    Guinness time!    (Shuts safe door and exits L., singing again.) |

|  |  |
|---|---|
|  | (Others come slowly on looking after her, mouths agape. They turn simultaneously to look at safe, back to where she has disappeared, then at each other.) |
| JACK | Come on! |
|  | (They rush at safe and open it. JACK takes out bag of money. Enter TOMMY L.) |
|  | Good. Now we'll put this in Dick's purse and then when old Fitzy finds the money gone you run in and say you saw Dick steal it. |
|  | (As he puts the money into DICK'S purse, TOMMY rushes at him and tries to stop him, clawing and biting him.) |
|  | Ow! Stop it, Tommy! |
|  | (TOMMY chases him round stage and JACK throws purse down by safe.) |
|  | OW! Come on, let's get out of here! |
|  | (TOMMY tries to stop them as they run to door, but they elude him and exit. He then tries to scrabble safe open with his paws. This is also unsuccessful so he picks up purse in his mouth, runs L. and 'MEOWS!' loudly to off L. Enter DICK and ALICE U.L.) |
| DICK | Hullo, Tommy, what's the matter? |
| ALICE | He's got your purse, Dick. |
| DICK | (taking it) Ah, I suppose you thought somebody might steal it, eh? I'm afraid there's not much in it to steal at the moment. |
| ALICE | Well, you'll be getting your first week's wages soon, Dick. |
|  | (Enter FITZWARREN R. with large account book.) |
| FITZWARREN | Come along, everybody, pay time. |
|  | (Moves down to safe, examining his book and ALICE crosses to him. SARAH enters L. at top speed and stops abruptly L. of safe.) |

| | |
|---|---|
| SARAH | Pay? How fortunate I just happened to be passing. |
| | (DICK moves into queue behind SARAH as JACK enters as unobtrusively as he can through door. TOMMY turns on him, hissing and arching his back.) |
| DICK | Tommy, you mustn't hiss at Jack like that. He hasn't done any harm. |
| | (TOMMY disagrees and DICK tries to quiet him. CAPTAIN and MATE enter through door and point at DICK.) |
| CAPTAIN | It was him. |
| MATE | We saw - |
| JACK | Ssh! Not yet. |
| CAP and MATE | Oh, sorry.   (They exit through door.) |
| FITZWARREN | Now, everybody here? Sarah, Jack, Dick? |
| ALICE | Yes, Father. |
| | (CAPTAIN and MATE re-enter and point at DICK.) |
| CAPTAIN | It was him. |
| MATE | We saw - |
| JACK | Not yet! |
| CAP and MATE | Oh, sorry.   (They retire to doorway and chat quietly.) |
| FITZWARREN | Right, now the money.   (Opens safe.)   Where is the money? It's gone! I've been robbed! |
| OTHERS | Robbed! |
| FITZWARREN | Yes, robbed! Who can have done it? |
| JACK | (trying frantically to attract the chatting CAPTAIN and MATE)   Come on! |
| FITZWARREN | (running to door)   We must get the police. No, they haven't been invented yet. Send for the Beadle! |
| | (CAPTAIN and MATE come to life as he reaches the door.) |

| | |
|---|---|
| CAP and MATE | It was – |
| FITZWARREN | Out of the way! |
| | (Pushes them aside and knocks them over.) |
| | I've been robbed! Call out the watch! Help! Help! (Dances back into shop.) Don't all stand there – do something! |
| | (CHORUS start hurrying on through shop door, preventing CAPTAIN and MATE from entering.) |
| CHORUS | What is it? What's wrong? What's wrong? What's the matter? |
| FITZWARREN | The matter! I've been robbed, that's what's the matter! |
| ALICE | Father, calm down. |
| FITZWARREN | CALM DOWN! I'll calm down when I find out who the thief is. |
| | (CAPTAIN and MATE manage to force their way in and point dramatically to DICK.) |
| CAP and MATE | It was him! We saw him steal it! |
| | (All eyes turn to DICK in C.) |
| ALICE, SARAH, FITZWARREN | Dick? |
| TOMMY | (frantically shakes head and points at JACK, CAPTAIN and MATE) |
| DICK | But I've never stolen anything in my life. And if you don't believe me here is my purse – look. |
| | (Turns it upside down – gasp of amazement from all as money falls out. JACK retreats. DICK is horrified and astounded.) |
| FITZWARREN | (picking up money) So, it was you. |
| ALICE | It must be a mistake. I know it must be a mistake. |
| FITZWARREN | Mistake! The mistake was mine for ever employing him. (To DICK.) Go! Leave my house immediately! |

(<u>MUSIC 21</u>   'AWAY, AWAY')

I trusted you, you stole from me.
Go, leave my house immediately.

**DICK**   To solve this mystery I must seek.
O sir, I pray you, let me speak.

**FITZWARREN**   I will not hear another word.

**CHORUS, JACK, CAP and MATE**   He will not hear another word.

**DICK**   O sir, I pray -

**FITZ, JACK, CH, CAP and MATE**       Away, away!

**ALICE**   O Father, I know in his eyes,
He would not stoop to deception and lies.

**SARAH, CHORUS**   O think of this youth.
In vain she pleads he is telling the truth.

**FITZWARREN**   Away, away!
I have nothing more to say.

(DICK sorrowfully picks up his bundle and stick and moves to door, followed by a very woebegone TOMMY. DICK turns back to ALICE.)

**DICK**   You're so lovely.

**DICK and ALICE**   I will ne'er forget you -

**FITZ, JACK, CH, CAP and MATE**   Away, away, away, away, away!

(All hands point accusingly at him. ALICE, in tears, turns to SARAH for comfort and over final bars of music as DICK and TOMMY turn to go, demonic peals of laughter from KING RAT are heard off L. and LIGHTS DIM to

BLACKOUT

Close traverse tabs. Fly in Scene 4 frontcloth, if used.)

PART I

Scene Four - ON THE WAY TO HIGHGATE HILL

(Frontcloth or tabs. Signpost painted in C. of cloth, reading 'TO HIGHGATE HILL' and pointing to L., or prop signpost set in C. during Blackout. If cloth is used, tabs to begin.)

(MUSIC 22   KING RAT's laughter continues as he enters L.)

KING RAT
The vict'ry's mine! My schemes succeed!
I've triumph'd both in word and deed!

(MUSIC 23   Enter FAIRY SILVERCHIME R.)

SILVERCHIME
For but a little ye have won,
But I shall ere the tale be done
Make this the very means whereby
My ward unto his goal shall fly.

KING RAT
A likely tale!

SILVERCHIME
Aye, 'tis and true.

KING RAT
If't please ye to such thoughts pursue,
Then think away. Ere long ye'll see
That thoughts no vict'ry wrest from me.

(Exit KING RAT L. and SILVERCHIME R. Open traverse tabs. LIGHTS UP.   MUSIC 24   Enter CAPTAIN and MATE R.)

CAPTAIN
Well, we've got old Fitzwarren to commission the ship. Now all we've got to do is find the ship again. (Sees signpost.)   Here, are you sure this is the right way to the docks?

MATE
Yes.

CAPTAIN
Seems funny to me. Going uphill to the docks. I mean, how do they keep all that water up there?

MATE
Maybe they're dry docks.

CAPTAIN
They were wet enough when we left 'em. I shall be very annoyed if they've gone and taken all that water away from the 'Saucy Sal'. She might fall over. I think we ought to ask somebody if we're going right.

| | |
|---|---|
| MATE | I did ask somebody. |
| CAPTAIN | Oh, and what did they say? |
| MATE | They said - yes, the docks were at the top of the hill right beside the stinging nettles. |
| CAPTAIN | Doh! Clot! Right beside the stinging nettles! You've brought us all this way for nothing and we've got a thousand and one things to do. We've got to provision the ship, overhaul her rigging, find a crew, and we've got to do all that sewing. |
| MATE | Sewing? |
| CAPTAIN | Yes, sewing. There's that nasty rent in the mainsail, where you stuck your toe through it. |
| MATE | That was your fault for using my sheet as a mainsail. You should use your own sheets. |
| CAPTAIN | Mine are no use. They're only single-bed size. And another thing - will you kindly stop using the lifeboat as a bath? |
| MATE | But it is the bath. |
| CAPTAIN | I know it is. But look what happened last time we did lifeboat drill - we were nearly drowned, because you'd left the plug out. But we must hurry up and find the docks. It's nearly lighting-up time and I didn't leave the 'Saucy Sal's' parking lights on. |
| | (They start to go R.) |
| MATE | Oo, I don't think we'd better go that way. I can see that Dick Whittington bloke coming. |
| CAPTAIN | Oh, dear, so he is. Well, where can we go? |
| MATE | I know - let's go and hide in the docks. |
| CAPTAIN | But we don't know where the docks are. |
| MATE | Yes, we do. Right beside the stinging nettles. |
| | (CAPTAIN chases MATE off L. Slight pause. MUSIC 25 Enter DICK R., very weary, followed by TOMMY.) |
| DICK | Well, we haven't come far, Tommy, but I'm tired already. Let's sit here and rest a little. |

1 - 4 - 48

(TOMMY agrees and they sit in C.)

**DICK** Do you know, Tommy, I trod this same road coming into London. I remember passing this signpost and thinking - 'it'll be some time before I pass you again'. And yet here I am just a few days later.

**TOMMY** (puts a comforting paw in DICK's lap)

**DICK** It seems a great deal longer than a few days, though; so much has happened. First I met you, then Alice, then I found a job, and then - (Sighs.) Well, I've still got you, anyway, Tommy.

**TOMMY** (nods and gently rubs head against him)

**DICK** But now the thing that worries me is - ought I to keep you?

**TOMMY** (looks up, puzzled)

**DICK** Well, I'm not much of a success, am I? I've been thinking maybe you ought to leave me and find yourself another master, who can look after you properly, and give you nice things to eat and a warm fire to curl youself up by at night and -

(Turns to TOMMY, who has started to wash himself.)

Are you listening to me, Tommy?

**TOMMY** (nods briefly and continues washing)

**DICK** Well, don't you think I'm right?

**TOMMY** (looks at him for a second then tosses head contemptuously)

**DICK** No, you can't dismiss it like that, Tommy. I've been thinking about it very hard as we came along and for your own sake, I'm afraid we must part. (Rises.) You go back to London and find yourself a nice comfortable home and I'll go on to Highgate Hill.

**TOMMY** (looks at him, astonished)

**DICK** Well - (Strokes TOMMY's head.)

|  |  |
|---|---|
|  | Goodbye, Tommy. (Picks up bundle, turns and walks away L.) |
| TOMMY | (rises and trots after him) Meow. |
| DICK | (stops) No, Tommy, you're going the wrong way. (Pulls an unwilling TOMMY to R.) You have to go this way, while I go this way. (Turns and walks L.) |
| TOMMY | (after a second, follows him to L.) Meow! |
| DICK | (stops) Tommy, I'm doing this for your own good and you're not being at all helpful. If you don't go at once I shall get very angry. (Pointing R.) Go on, go away. |
| TOMMY | (looks at him, helpless) |
| DICK | Go on! Don't you understand, I don't want you any more. |
| TOMMY | (hangs head, then turns slowly and slinks R. Stops to look back and very quietly:) Meow. |
|  | (But DICK shakes head and motions him to R. and he continues very unhappily to R.) |
| DICK | Tommy! |
| TOMMY | (stops and turns hopefully) |
| DICK | Goodbye, Tommy. (Waves.) |
| TOMMY | (waves a mournful paw back and exits R.) |
| DICK | Poor Tommy. I didn't really want to do that - he's the only friend I've got left, but I'm sure I was right to send him away - well, I hope I was - and yet - and yet - (Shrugs, sighs and turns to go.) Well, he's gone now, but oh! I do wish he wasn't. |
| TOMMY | (bounds joyfully on) MEOW! |
|  | (Close traverse tabs slowly. Fly out frontcloth.) |
| DICK | Tommy! You bad cat, thank goodness you disobeyed me. (Kneels and strokes him.) What a fool I am, of course I can't do without you and I'll never try to part with you again. It's just that I was depressed, but I don't feel so bad |

|  |  |
|---|---|
|  | now. In fact, I shouldn't be surprised if things don't get better soon. Come on, Tommy, on to Highgate Hill. |
| TOMMY | (nods happily) |
|  | (As they move R. - <u>MUSIC 26.</u>) |
|  | BLACKOUT |
|  | (Open traverse tabs.) |

PART I

Scene Five - HIGHGATE HILL

(Full set. Cut-out ground row at back of rostrum showing distant London skyline. Rostrum as a grass bank with leaves scattered over it. Below rostrum a milestone marked 'LONDON, 5 MILES'. Woodwings L. and R. <u>EFFECT 10.</u> Motor car noises and hooting off R. <u>MUSIC 27.</u> A rather peculiar-looking car, driven by SARAH with FITZWARREN as passenger, enters very slowly R. It has a picnic basket on the back.)

SARAH      Oh dear, Jemima's a bit sluggish today.

(FITZWARREN stops R.C. and his end of the car stops with him. SARAH, with her end, continues to L.)

Ah, that's better.

FITZWARREN      Just look at the view up here. Beautiful! Beautiful! What a pity I can't see it.

(<u>EFFECT 11.</u> Car backfires.)

SARAH      Now then! (Stops her end of car R.C. by applying the outside brake, which comes off in her hand.) Oh dear. (Turns.) I say, Fitzy - Oh, he's gone. Aah! Where have you got to? (Looks frantically round and gets out.)

FITZWARREN      Nowhere. I'm still here in the back of the car. Oh. (Moves his piece over to other.) You know, I don't think this car's quite what it used to be. (Gets out and fixes two ends together.)

SARAH      You're telling me. You know the brake?

FITZWARREN      Yes.

SARAH      (holding it up) Well, now it's a broke. (Throws it off L. and leans on bonnet.)

FITZWARREN      We'll have to leave the car in gear then.

SARAH      We can't. The gear lever came off five miles back.

(Radiator starts gushing steam. Powder bulb.)

Dear me, I'd better take a look at Jemima's engine. (Opens bonnet.) Are you all right, engine?

|  |  |
|---|---|
|  | (JACK's head appears in bonnet.) |
| JACK | No, I'm not. I'm thoroughly overheated. |
| SARAH | Yes, you do look a bit red in the face. |
| JACK | Well, this hill's enough to make any engine pink. |
| SARAH | Ooh! You must be very tired, dear. You'd better have a little nap. |
|  | (JACK falls asleep. Audience shout. JACK wakes.) |
|  | I didn't mean in the engine, dear. You get out and lay down while we get the picnic ready. |
| JACK | Righto. |
|  | (Gets out of car. FITZWARREN takes picnic basket from car and hands it to SARAH, who places it D.C.) |
|  | Wake me up when it's ready. |
|  | (Lies down below basket, which SARAH is opening to take out a table-cloth.) |
| SARAH | Lay the cloth out first, Fitzy. |
|  | (FITZWARREN takes cloth and lays it over JACK.) |
| JACK | (dreamily)   Short back and sides, please. (Falls asleep.) |
| FITZWARREN | (to SARAH)   Pardon? |
| SARAH | Granted. |
|  | (FITZWARREN looks confused as SARAH bends to look in basket, <u>EFFECT 12.</u> Buzzing noise.) |
| FITZWARREN | Ooh, a wasp.   (Follows the wasp with his eyes from L. to C. till it lands on SARAH's behind. Buzzing stops.) |
| SARAH | Now, here are the plates. |
|  | (As she lifts them out, FITZWARREN smacks hard at the wasp on its resting place.) |
|  | (Straightening up and dropping plates.)   Aah! |
|  | (<u>EFFECT 13.</u> Buzzing.) |

| | |
|---|---|
| FITZWARREN | Missed. |
| SARAH | You certainly did not miss. How dare you, Mr Fitzwarren? |
| FITZWARREN | It was a wasp. |
| SARAH | A wasp? Oh, I'll soon deal with that.  (She lunges out at it once or twice with plate, breakable, then chases it balletically round stage. She stops as she sees it touch down on FITZ-WARREN's head. Buzzing stops.)  Ah! (Tiptoes D.S., raises plate and crashes it on the unsuspecting FITZWARREN's head.) |
| FITZWARREN | WAH! |
| SARAH | Got it! |
| FITZWARREN | (takes wasp in fingers with one hand and sorrowfully rubs head with other)  You got me, too. |
| SARAH | (bends to examine wasp)  Wait a minute, that's not our wasp. It's got a different coloured jersey on. |
| | (EFFECT 14. Buzzing, then MUSIC 'ting' and SARAH clutches her behind. Buzzing stops.) |
| | Ouch! That was ours though. I say, where's Jack? |
| FITZWARREN | (peers round shortsightedly)  I don't know, can't see him anywhere. |
| SARAH | Well, we'll just have to start without him. |
| | (They kneel down.) |
| | Oh, I say, you have chosen a bumpy place, Fitzy. Never mind. Here's the loaf.  (Hands FITZ-WARREN long prop French loaf, hitting him in face as she does so.)  So sorry. And here's the ham.  (Takes large prop ham from basket.) |
| | (EFFECT 15. Buzzing.) |
| | Look out! The wasp's back! Quick, there it is! |
| | (Buzzing stops. SARAH aims at JACK's toes with ham and FITZWARREN likewise with loaf and then continue along the length of him.) |

1 - 5 - 54

| | | |
|---|---|---|
| JACK | ⎫ (together) | Ow! <u>Ow!</u> OW! <u>OW!</u> |
| FITZ and SARAH | ⎭ | Missed! <u>Missed!</u> MISSED! <u>MISSED!</u> |

(JACK sits up indignantly.)

FITZWARREN      Ah, there you are, Jack.

JACK      What are you playing at?

SARAH      We were having a bit of trouble from a wasp, Jack.

JACK      You'll be having a bit of trouble from me if you go on like that.

(JACK gets clear of cloth and he and FITZWARREN spread it on ground.)

Is everything ready?

SARAH      Yes, I'm just getting out the eats. Here's a nice custard pie.

(Gives it to FITZWARREN who passes it to JACK.)

And a trifle.      (Gives it to FITZWARREN.)
And a lovely blankymangy.

(<u>EFFECT 16.</u> Buzzing.)

Look out! The wasp!

(They watch wasp approach from L.)

Duck!

(They duck, quickly moving the three puddings to one side away from their faces, as wasp dive-bombs over them. Buzzing stops. They sit up.)

SARAH      (to Audience)      Ah, you thought we were going to -

(<u>EFFECT 17.</u> Buzzing.)

FITZWARREN      (looking to R.)      Duck!

(They duck, again moving puddings away. Buzzing stops. They sit up.)

SARAH      Fooled you ag-

(<u>EFFECT 18.</u> Buzzing.)

JACK      (looking to L.)      Duck!

|              | (They duck. JACK and FITZWARREN land in their puddings, SARAH moves hers away again. Buzzing stops. They sit up.) |
|---|---|
| SARAH | And ag-   (Sees JACK and FITZWARREN.) Oh.   (Starts to laugh and laughs more and more, rocking to and fro. <u>EFFECT 19.</u> Buzzing. She gives a little shriek and falls backwards upsetting blancmange over her face. Buzzing stops. She sits up, to the amusement of JACK and FITZ-WARREN.)   Well, really! Come on, let's go home.   (Starts packing up.) |
| JACK | (helping her)   Yes, let's. I'm fed up with this picnic lark. |
| FITZWARREN | (also helping)   So am I. I don't really like picnics anyway. I much prefer a proper meal. (Puts basket on back of car.) |
| SARAH | Yes, do you know, the last time I went on a picnic all I had to eat was a rock cake and a roll. |
| FITZ and JACK | Ah, rock 'n' roll! |
| SARAH | How old fashioned. |
|  | (<u>MUSIC 28</u>  'THIRTY-TWO BAR ROCK') |
| ALL | Here's a silly sort of song That is exactly thirty-two bars long, And it goes umty-tumty-tumty-tum, 'Cos rock 'n' roll's the idiom. |
|  | Here's a song for sevenpence, Of which the words don't make the slightest sense. So if you want a pointless song to sing, Rock 'n' roll's the very thing. |
|  | Fa la la, hey nonny no, Boop-a-doop and vodeodo, Hi-de-hi, hip hooray - Aren't we having fun today! |
|  | There's eight bars left to end this song, Which, as we said, is thirty-two bars long; And now at last we have achieved our goal - We've sung a song in rock 'n' roll. |

1 - 5 - 56

(As number ends FITZWARREN and SARAH get in car and they exit L., with JACK pushing at back. Slight pause. LIGHTS DIM. MUSIC 29. FAIRY SPOT UP. Enter FAIRY SILVERCHIME R.)

SILVERCHIME  Come, faithful cat.

(TOMMY trots on R. FAIRY indicates bank at back of stage.)

There must ye sleep.
And ere the dawn o'er night doth creep,
Thy master's courage I'll renew
With visions sweet and fresh as dew.
So gather leaves to make a bed,
That Dick may rest his weary head.

(TOMMY bows low. Exit SILVERCHIME R. MUSIC 30. TOMMY moves up and jumps onto bank and starts to arrange leaves into a pillow. One leaf gives him some trouble, necessitating some chasing and playing with it in a cat-like manner. Leaf attached to a thin line running off stage. Finally it falls over edge of bank. He tosses head impatiently and jumps down to retrieve it, then places it on top of pillow. Tries the pillow for comfort, shakes head, very disdainfully removes the troublesome leaf, tries pillow again and is satisfied.)

DICK  (off R.)  Tommy! Tommy!  (Enter R.) Ah, there you are, Tommy. What have you been up to?

TOMMY  (proudly indicates bedding arrangements)

DICK  Oh, Tommy, you've made the beds. You are a clever cat.

TOMMY  (modestly agrees)

(DICK sits on bank, TOMMY sits beside him and DICK undoes his bundle. LIGHTS COMMENCE FADE.)

DICK  Before we go to sleep we'd better have some supper. I'm jolly hungry, are you?

TOMMY  (nods emphatically)

| | |
|---|---|
| DICK | Let's see, what have we got?  (Taking them out.) A crust of bread and - another crust of bread. Well, we'd better leave one of them for breakfast. (Replaces one crust and looks at very small crust left.)  Hmm.  We-ll, I don't think I really feel so hungry after all, do you? |
| TOMMY | (nods, then hurriedly shakes head) |
| DICK | (breaks crust in two and gives half to TOMMY) Here you are, Tommy.

(Both put their halves in their mouths simultaneously.)

Um, excellent.

(TOMMY nods. They chew for a moment, then swallow. DICK brushes hands together and wipes his mouth.)

Well, that's supper over. So nice not having to waste a lot of time eating, isn't it? |
| TOMMY | (nods half-hearted agreement) |
| DICK | It's such a lovely night, I don't really feel like going to sleep yet, do you? |
| TOMMY | (nods decidedly and curls up to go to sleep) |
| DICK | (laughs and lies back)  All right.  Goodnight, Tommy. |
| TOMMY | Meow.

(Pause. DICK sits up clasping knees with hands.) |
| DICK | I say, Tommy. |
| TOMMY | (raises head) |
| DICK | Did you like Alice? |
| TOMMY | (nods and lies down) |
| DICK | I'm glad.  (Pause.)  I liked her very much, you know. |
| TOMMY | (raises head, nods and lies down)

(Pause.) |

| | |
|---|---|
| DICK | I wonder if I'll ever see her again? |
| TOMMY | (looks up, nods very emphatically and lies down) |
| DICK | You think so? How can you be so sure? |
| TOMMY | (struggles laboriously up, points at DICK, puts a hushing paw to lips, cradles head on paws, points to DICK's pillow and lies down again) |
| DICK | (laughs)  Very well, Tommy, I can take a hint. (Lies back yawning.)  Night-night, pleasant dreams. |
| TOMMY | (murmurs) |
| DICK | (sleepily)  Pleasant dreams. |
| | (LIGHTS COMPLETE THEIR FADE. MUSIC 31. FAIRY SPOT UP.  Enter FAIRY SILVERCHIME R.) |
| SILVERCHIME | Sleep, sleep. And ere the weary night is through, I'll show thee dreams to make thy dreams come true. |
| | (Enter CHORUS as FAIRIES L. and R.  MUSIC 32. Mime ballet, led by SILVERCHIME, foretelling fame and fortune for DICK and reunion with ALICE. Towards end of ballet, dawn begins to break and bells start to peal. FAIRIES exit. SILVERCHIME moves behind DICK.) |
| | Awake! And hear the bells peal thy renown! Awake! And turn ye back to London Town! |
| | (Exit SILVERCHIME R. DICK sits up, stretching and yawning. We hear the voices singing off, very faintly at first and growing in volume during scene.) |
| VOICES | (off)  Turn again, Whittington, Thou worthy citizen, Lord Mayor of London! |
| DICK | What a beautiful morning. Wake up, Tommy, wake up! It's a lovely day. |
| TOMMY | (wakes unwillingly and stretches cat-like) |
| DICK | I had such a wonderful dream, Tommy. I dreamt I was very rich and that Alice was going to marry |

|  |  |
|---|---|
|  | me and that I was Lord Mayor of London. That's funny, can you hear those bells, Tommy? They seem to be saying Lord Mayor of London. Listen - |
| TOMMY | (sits up listening, then listens more eagerly) |
| DICK | (excited, jumping up)   Listen, they're calling to me - Turn again, Whittington, Lord Mayor of London. Can you hear them, Tommy? |
| TOMMY | (nods, and jumps up and down in his excitement) |
| DICK | (half-whispered)   It could be true, it could be true. You never get anywhere if you run away from things.   (Triumphantly.)   I will go back! (Gathers up bundle and stick and puts hat on at jaunty angle.)   Come on, Tommy, we're going back! Back to London, to try again! |

(MUSIC mounts to crescendo and CURTAIN DESCENDS with DICK, stick and bundle on shoulder, TOMMY standing eagerly beside him, gazing towards London. CURTAIN RISES on same picture, with the addition of SILVERCHIME and FAIRIES.)

CURTAIN


<u>MUSIC 33</u>   ENTR'ACTE

## PART II

### Scene Six - THE DOCKS AT WAPPING

(Full set. At L. side of rostrum a movable cut-out of the stern of the 'Saucy Sal', set at half the depth of rostrum. In front of it a cut-out wall, about 2 ft. high and 'L' shaped, the long arm of the 'L' running offstage to L. and the short arm running U.S. at C. to meet cut-out wall running along back of rostrum from C. to R. In the 'Saucy Sal' some portholes are cut out and there is an opening from which a gang-plank slopes to D.S. edge of rostrum where there are steps down to stage. A rudder leans against gang-plank. Shop wing R. - 'SHIP'S CHANDLER' - which has a plank of wood leaning against it. L. wing an inn with practical door and sign - 'YE OLDE WAPPING ARMS. Best Wapping Wallop on Draught'.

CAPTAIN and MATE discovered with CHORUS, some of whom are SAILORS loading cargo onto ship, and others their GIRL FRIENDS. MUSIC 34 'HEAVE HO!')

| | |
|---|---|
| ALL | Heave ho! and our course is fine, <br> And the yards are set to a running line. |
| CAP and MATE | It's words like these to landlubbers all, <br> And even to us, mean nothing at all! |
| ALL | Heave ho! for the seven seas, <br> And lots of salty sounds like these; <br> But of all the nautical words we know, <br> The ones we like best are 'Yo Heave Ho!' |
| GIRLS | We are gathered here to send a <br> Greeting from the feminine gender. <br> We hope our men enjoy the trip, <br> And try very hard not to sink the ship. <br> After 'Yo Heave Ho, and a bottle of rum', <br> We girls are going home to Mum. <br> Of all the sea-songs ever wrote <br> This one's the first all on one note! |
| ALL | Heave ho! for the watch below, <br> And just for luck, another Heave ho! |
| CAP and MATE | And in case you think that's all we can say, <br> We've an extra verse for Saturday. |
| ALL | Heave ho! for the seven bells <br> When we're dress'd up we're the ocean swells. |

|          | And we're bound to say, lest you don't know, |
|          | The name of this shanty's 'Yo Heave Ho!' |

CAPTAIN  Now, me hearties, are you all fit and ready?

CHORUS  Aye, aye, Cap'n.

CAPTAIN  That's the spirit. Oh, it's a hard life aboard ship. Many's the time you'll be out there with the 'Saucy Sal' rolling in a running sea, the wind tearing at the rigging and the spray blowing in your face, while you're lashed to the wheel, trying to hold her to her course, but it's a man's life, shipmates, and when you're in port again you'll be as proud as I am to say you've sailed the Seven Seas in the 'Saucy Sal'.    (Ends in dramatic pose.)

MATE  What are you talking about? We've never been further than Southend before.

CAPTAIN  Shurrup! Now, me lucky lads, off you go and kiss you wives and sweethearts goodbye. We sail with the Daz - I mean, the Surf - the tide!

CHORUS  Aye, aye, Cap'n.

(CHORUS exit variously. MATE picks up rudder from gang-plank.)

MATE  I say, what's this?

CAPTAIN  Doh! What's that! That's the rudder.

MATE  Oh. Well, where does it go?

CAPTAIN  Where do you think it goes? On the end, of course.

MATE  Oh, right.    (Turns to go, then turns back.)
Er - which end?

CAPTAIN  Which end? The <u>rudder</u> end.

MATE  The other end to what?

CAPTAIN  No, no, rudder, not other.

MATE  Oh, not the other end.

CAPTAIN  No. Er - Yes. Well - it's the other end to the end which isn't the rudder end.

MATE  Is that this end or that end?

| | | |
|---|---|---|
| CAPTAIN | | No, it's the rudder end. Anyway, it depends which way you're going, which end you have it. |
| MATE | | Oh, let's throw it away. It's not important, is it? |
| CAPTAIN | | It's very important. And you've got me confused now. Oh well, mark it sharp end, and we'll put it on later. |

(MATE places rudder in ship.)

| | | |
|---|---|---|
| FITZWARREN | | (off R.)   Jack! Jack! |
| CAPTAIN | | Ah, here comes the owner. Stand by to pipe him aboard. |

(MATE looks at him, shrugs and takes out a pipe and lights it as FITZWARREN enters R. laden down with two large kitbags and a big box marked - 'KWELLS'.)

| | | |
|---|---|---|
| FITZWARREN | | Jack! Sarah! Oh, where have they got to? Leaving me to carry all their luggage. |
| CAPTAIN | | (saluting)   Mr Fitzwarren, sir! |
| FITZWARREN | | What? Oh - you, you. I mean, aye, aye. (Tries to return salute and drops a kitbag on his toe.)   Ouch! |
| CAPTAIN | | And welcome to the 'Saucy Sal'. |

(Claps FITZWARREN so heartily on back he drops other kitbag onto other foot.)

| | | |
|---|---|---|
| FITZWARREN | | Ow! |

(MATE starts blowing smoke from pipe into FITZWARREN's face causing him to break into a fit of coughing.)

Here! What are you playing at?

| | | |
|---|---|---|
| MATE | | I'm piping you aboard. |
| CAPTAIN | | No, no, no. Not that kind of pipe. |
| FITZWARREN | | Everything all right, Captain? |
| CAPTAIN | | Yes, sir. Except I'm a bit short of crew. |
| FITZWARREN | | Oh, that's all right, I'm sending Jack and Sarah with you. That is, I would be if I hadn't lost them |

|   |   |
|---|---|
|   | on the way here. |
|   | (Enter JACK and SARAH in auditorium. FITZWARREN, CAPTAIN and MATE move down to floats during following.) |
| SARAH | Oh yes, I think we're right now, Jack. This is the docks. |
| JACK | It doesn't look like the docks to me. All these people sitting down. |
| SARAH | That's just the way dock-workers work. I expect they're enjoying a nice quiet strike. Oh look, I can see the 'Saucy Sal'. |
| JACK | Oh, yes.     (To lady in Audience.)     Hello, Sal. |
| SARAH | No, no, no. Not that lady. |
| FITZWARREN | So there you are. |
| CAPTAIN | What are you doing down there? |
| JACK | We were looking for you. |
| SARAH | But it's so nice down here I think we'll stay, don't you, Jack? |
| JACK | Yes, let's. |
| FITZWARREN | But you can't do that. |
| JACK, SARAH | (sitting on steps at foot of cat-walk)    Oh yes, we can. |
| CAPTAIN | In that case, we'll go down and fetch 'em up. |
| FITZ and MATE | Yes. |
|   | (FITZWARREN, CAPTAIN and MATE exit D.S. on whichever side leads to a pass door.) |
| SARAH | Come on, let's fool 'em and go up on top. |
|   | (SARAH and JACK move over cat-walk onto stage as CAPTAIN, MATE and FITZWARREN enter through pass door.) |
| JACK, SARAH | Coo-ee! |
| FITZWARREN | Back again! |
|   | (They run back through pass door.) |

| | |
|---|---|
| SARAH | Down again! |

(SARAH and JACK run back over cat-walk into auditorium. FITZWARREN, CAPTAIN and MATE run onstage.)

| | |
|---|---|
| JACK, SARAH | Coo-ee! |
| SARAH | Bet you can't catch us! |

(JACK and SARAH run up aisle and out at the back of the auditorium. FITZWARREN, CAPTAIN and MATE pound over cat-walk and after them with much ad-lib shouting and by-play with Audience. Just as they are about to go out, JACK and SARAH appear at entrance on other side of auditorium.)

| | |
|---|---|
| JACK, SARAH | Coo-ee! |

(Their pursuers double back down aisle and across a transverse aisle to get to them, but they disappear and re-appear where they left auditorium just as the others are about to run out again.)

Coo-ee!

(FITZWARREN, CAPTAIN and MATE turn back and return along transverse aisle as JACK and SARAH run out through pass door. They do likewise and JACK and SARAH immediately return through it into auditorium.)

| | |
|---|---|
| SARAH | Fooled 'em!    (To Audience.)    Now look, when they run on up there you all shout, 'Coo-ee!' with us. Stand by. |
| JACK, SARAH | (leading Audience)    Coo-ee! |
| CAPTAIN | Oh, it's not fair. |
| MATE | I'm not going to play any more. |
| FITZWARREN | (very breathless)    Neither am I. In fact, I can't play any more. |
| JACK | I could do with a rest myself. |
| SARAH | Then we'd better go up before you fall asleep. |

(JACK falls asleep and is awakened by Audience

|   |   |
|---|---|
| | shout. SARAH and JACK ad-lib goodbyes to Audience and cross cat-walk onto stage.) |
| FITZWARREN | Well, now you've arrived at last, you'd better report for duty and settle in.  (Moving to inn.) I'm going to start checking the cargo. |
| CAPTAIN | But the cargo's not in the Wapping Arms, Mr Fitzwarren. |
| FITZWARREN | I know, but this is a better place for checking, the er - the light's better in here.  (Exit into inn.) |
| SARAH | I bet the brown's better in there, too. Well, here we are, Captain. Can we see our rooms? |
| CAPTAIN | Rooms? You don't have a room on a ship, you have a cabin. |
| SARAH | A cab in what? |
| CAPTAIN | You don't have a cab in anything. On a ship a cabin is a room. |
| JACK, SARAH | Oh-hh. |
| JACK | Anyway, I hope you've got me a nice comfy bed. |
| CAPTAIN | Not bed - bunk. |
| | (SARAH and JACK run to R.) |
| | Oi! Where are you going? |
| | (They stop.) |
| JACK | You told us to bunk. |
| CAPTAIN | I did not. A bunk's a bed, same as what a cabin's a room. |
| JACK, SARAH | Oh-hh. |
| CAPTAIN | Now stop mucking about and get aboard. |
| | (SARAH and JACK look at each other then, seeking plank U.R., fetch it and throw it at CAPTAIN's feet.) |
| | Doh!  (Picks it up and testily hands it to MATE.) I didn't want you to get <u>a</u> board. To get aboard means to get on the ship. |
| JACK, SARAH | Oh-hh. |

| | |
|---|---|
| CAPTAIN | There's a few things you'd better learn. On a ship, the stairs are companion-ways, the doors are hatches, the floors are decks, the kitchen's a galley and the dining-room's a mess. |
| JACK, SARAH | Well, clean it up then. |
| CAPTAIN | It doesn't need cleaning up! Don't you understand any nautical parlance? |
| SARAH | Certainly not. I'm never naughty in the parlour. |
| CAPTAIN | I give up. Blimey, what a crew! Get your kitbags and get aboard that ship. |
| JACK, SARAH | Right. |
| | (They pick up their kitbags and fling them, JACK over his L. and SARAH over her R. shoulder, so that they hit the CAPTAIN, who is between them and knock him over.) |
| CAPTAIN | Look out! Oh, you are careless. |
| JACK, SARAH | Sorry. (They move up steps onto rostrum.) |
| SARAH | Er - what did you just tell us to do? |
| CAPTAIN | Get aboard! |
| MATE | They can't. I've got the board. |
| CAPTAIN | Aah! Don't you start! (Chases others off into ship.) |
| JACK | (off) Wait a minute, I've forgotten the Kwells. (Runs out from ship and falls off end of gang-plank.) Ow! What a silly place to put a lot of nothing. |
| | (Picks himself up and limps over to 'KWELLS' box. Takes it back to ship and just as he is at R. of gang-plank enter ALICE R. below rostrum carrying a large scroll of paper.) |
| ALICE | Jack! |
| JACK | (trips over gang-plank) Alice! (Rises.) Oh, I am pleased to see you, Alice. (Steps forward off rostrum, falls and goes head over heels to land upright by her side.) Have a Kwell? |

ALICE  Er - no, thank you. I'm looking for father. He's forgotten the cargo list.

JACK  Oh, he's in there.

(ALICE moves towards inn.)

But don't go, Alice. There's something I want to tell you. Let me take it for you, then you can stay here and talk to me while I'm gone.  (Starts to go and stops.)  Oh no, that's no good. I shouldn't know what I was saying to you. You see it's about me. I - I'm in love, with - with - well, I'll describe her to you and you can try and guess who it is.

ALICE  All right.

JACK  She's a girl.

ALICE  Yes.

JACK  And she's got eyes - and lips.

ALICE  What colour?

JACK  Red eyes and blue lips. No. Blue eyes and red lips. Have you guessed yet?

ALICE  I think I guessed a long time ago, Jack. But I'm afraid she doesn't love you.

JACK  Oh. She's supposed to, you know. Something's gone wrong somewhere.

ALICE  She likes you very much, though.

JACK  That's nice - but it's not quite the same, is it?

(MUSIC 35  'SOMEBODY LOVING ME')

It's nice to know that everybody likes me;
   It's nice to hear them say they think I'm swell;
But ev'ry now and then a little thought comes up
        and strikes me,
   That I'd like somebody loving me as well.

I'm popular with puppydogs and babies;
   At all the Church bazaars I ring the bell;
But all the girls avoid me just as if I had the rabies;
   O, I'd like somebody loving me as well.

I know lots of games to play.
On 'Ring-a-ring-a-roses' I go gay;
But if I say, 'Please marry me',
One, two, three and out goes she.

I often feel like little Jackie Horner,
    Or Humpty Dumpty just before he fell;
But what's the use, when Spring is waiting round the
                           corner? -
    O, I'd like somebody loving me as well.

(They exit L. Enter CAPTAIN from ship, carrying two marlinspikes.)

| | |
|---|---|
| CAPTAIN | Wilfrid! |
| MATE | (off)   Yes?   (Enter from ship.)   I've just been fixing that rudder on. |
| CAPTAIN | Well, I hope you fixed it nice and firm. We don't want it waggling about. But I've got another problem now. Come here. |
| | (MATE goes to him.) |
| | I haven't got enough hands. |
| MATE | Well, you can't have mine. They're fixtures. |
| CAPTAIN | I'm talking about men - sailors. We still need some more of 'em, so we're going to shanghai 'em. |
| MATE | But won't it take rather a long time to get to Shanghai? |
| CAPTAIN | Oh, you are hignorant. What I mean is - when we see a bloke coming we go and hide and then when I say 'Now', we creep out and bonk him with these marlinspikes. That's called shanghaiing, see? |
| MATE | Oh. |
| CAPTAIN | (glances R.)    Here comes a bloke now. (Giving MATE a marlinspike.)    Quick, take this and hide over there.    (Points R.)    I'll hide over here.    (Indicates L.) |
| | (They run and hide as DICK and TOMMY enter R.) |
| DICK | Well, Tommy, how would you like to be a sea-going cat? |

| | |
|---|---|
| TOMMY | (considers and nods approval) |
| DICK | That's good, because we've tried to get work everywhere else in London without any luck, so the docks are our last chance. And you never know, we might get a pleasant surprise here. |
| CAPTAIN | (puts head on. In hoarse whisper:)  Now!<br>(Runs on tiptoe towards DICK, marlinspike at the ready.) |
| MATE }<br>TOMMY } | (together)  (popping head on)  Now?<br>(sensing danger)  Meow! |
| | (DICK turns towards CAPTAIN as TOMMY jumps across him and butts CAPTAIN in stomach. DICK grabs marlinspike from CAPTAIN's hand as he doubles up. MATE, having started out late, is just in time to be hit by marlinspike as DICK swings it back preparatory to hitting CAPTAIN. TOMMY leaps on top of CAPTAIN, and DICK holds MATE down with a foot.) |
| DICK | Well done, Tommy, we nearly got a very <u>un</u>pleasant surprise.<br><br>(CAPTAIN and MATE come round, rubbing their heads.) |
| CAPTAIN | Ooh, where am I? Who put this animated hearth-rug on top of me? |
| TOMMY | (hisses and spits and threatens to scratch his face with a paw) |
| CAPTAIN | No! I didn't mean that, I take it back! |
| DICK | Hullo, I recognise you two. You're the ones who accused me of stealing. |
| MATE | Cor! It's Dick Whittington! |
| DICK | What do you think you're playing at this time? |
| CAPTAIN | Well, we were trying to shanghai you, 'cos I'm short of men for my ship, the 'Saucy Sal'. |
| DICK | You're short of men? But I'm looking for a job at sea. Why didn't you just ask me to join your crew? |

| | |
|---|---|
| CAPTAIN | There, we never thought of that. Well, if you want a job, I've give you one. In fact, just to show there's no nasty feelings, I'll make you Second Mate. |
| DICK | Splendid! And what about the animated hearthrug? |
| CAPTAIN | He can be Second and a half Mate. |
| DICK | Good. Second and a half Mate, Tommy, let your Captain up. |
| | (TOMMY obediently jumps off CAPTAIN and salutes him as he rises. DICK lets MATE up.) |
| | When do we sail, Captain? |
| CAPTAIN | As soon as we've repaired out heads.     (Crossing to inn.)    Come on, Wilfrid, let's get a blood confusion. |
| MATE | (following)    But this isn't a hospital. They won't have any blood here. |
| CAPTAIN | Oh yes, they will. Nelson's Blood. |
| MATE | What's that? |
| CAPTAIN | Rum. |
| | (They exit into inn.) |
| DICK | We're in luck's way, Tommy. There's only one thing I could wish for now - to say goodbye to Alice. |
| | (Enter ALICE above inn.) |
| | Alice! |
| ALICE | Dick! |
| BOTH | What are you doing here? |
| | (They laugh and run into each other's arms, while TOMMY, with ostentatious tact, creeps off R.) |
| ALICE | Oh, I'm so glad to see you again, Dick. |
| DICK | And I was just this very second wishing to see you again. I wanted to say goodbye before I set sail. You see, I've just been made Second Mate on the 'Saucy Sal'. |

| | |
|---|---|
| ALICE | The 'Saucy Sal'? But that's the ship father's commissioned for a trading voyage. |
| DICK | What? I'd better keep out of his way then. Alice, I didn't get a chance to say this when — when I was turned out — but I didn't steal that money. |
| ALICE | I never thought you did, Dick. |
| DICK | Thank you, Alice, that's all that really matters to me. And one day, when I get back from this voyage, I shall come and ask you to be my wife. Till then, please go on believing in me. |
| ALICE | I shall always believe in you, Dick — because, you see, I love you. |

(MUSIC 36 'STAY THIS LOVE')

Love is the lamp that lightens my way;
The golden dawn of the day
    Deep within me glowing.

| | |
|---|---|
| DICK | Love is the beauty born in a song; A something supple and strong     As a river flowing. |
| BOTH | Stay lock'd within my breast, Never let me rest;     Stay this love for ever. |
| DICK | You are my soul that skyward must soar; The whispered sigh of the word 'evermore';     You are the dream divine.     Stay, this love of mine. |
| BOTH | Stay lock'd within my breast, Never let me rest;     Stay this love for ever. |
| ALICE | You are my soul that skyward must soar; The whispered sigh of the word 'evermore'; |
| BOTH |     You are the dream divine.     Stay, this love of mine. |

(They finish D.R.C. Enter CAPTAIN and MATE from inn.)

| | |
|---|---|
| CAPTAIN | (as they enter)     Come on, me hearties, shore |

|  |  |
|---|---|
|  | leave's up. |
| MATE | (crossing and calling off R.) Come on, you landscrubbers, all aboard. |
|  | (CHORUS drift on L. and R., to say goodbye to each other.) |
| DICK | Alice, I must go. Think of me, Alice. |
| ALICE | I will - for always. |
|  | (They embrace, TOMMY runs on R. and joins DICK. SARAH pops her head through a porthole, looking rather green. GREEN SPOT onto her.) |
| SARAH | Are we nearly there, yet? |
| CAPTAIN | Don't be silly - we haven't started. |
| SARAH | Oh dear. (Disappears.) |
|  | (Enter FITZWARREN from inn, smacking lips.) |
| FITZWARREN | Well, that's got the cargo checked. |
| CAPTAIN | Now then, me hearties, all aboard and off we go. |
| DICK and CHORUS | (saluting) Aye, aye! |
| TOMMY | (saluting) Meow, meow! |
|  | (DICK and TOMMY move onto ship. FITZWARREN crosses to ALICE. JACK runs on L.) |
| JACK | Oi! Wait for me! |
| CAPTAIN | Hurry up, then. All hands stand by to weigh anchor and cast off! |
|  | (SARAH reappears at top of gangway.) |
|  | (<u>MUSIC 37</u> 'OUT TO SEA' Words and Music - John Crocker, arranged by Eric Gilder.) |
| CAP, MATE, JACK, DICK, SARAH, CHORUS | Farewell, we must go, for the tide is a-running, you know, We don't want to go, but the wind out to sea does blow; And time and tide will brook no delay, We wish we could, but we cannot stay. Haul up the anchor, let's get under way - Out to sea! |

| | |
|---|---|
| ALICE and<br>GIRLS | We smile our goodbye, but the wind is a-blinding<br>       our eye,<br>And we always sigh ev'ry time from our arms they<br>       fly. |
| ALL | But men must earn their living some way,<br>For the most of life is work not play.<br>Haul up the anchor, let's get under way -<br> Out to sea!<br><br>We live on the sea, for the sea is our living, you<br>       see,<br>We don't love the sea, and we don't think the sea<br>       loves we,<br>But the sails are set and we're away<br>To the whistling wind and the stinging spray.<br>Make fast the anchor, for we're under way -<br> Out to sea!<br>Out to sea! Out to sea! Out to sea!<br> Out to sea! |

(During last verse SAILORS of CHORUS, CAPTAIN, MATE and JACK get on ship and as number ends, the ship starts to move slowly off L., moved by the actors. The voyagers exchange shouted goodbyes with the others.)

BLACKOUT

(Close traverse tabs. Fly in Scene 7 frontcloth, if used.)

PART II

Scene Seven - 'TWEEN DECKS

(Frontcloth or tabs. Tabs to begin if cloth is used. GREEN FLASH L.
GREEN SPOT UP. <u>MUSIC 38</u>. Enter KING RAT L.)

KING RAT      Aha!
Things turn out better than I'd thought,
For she who hoped my scheme to thwart,
Instead hath placed Dick in my net.
Once out to sea their course is set
A mighty tempest I shall brew,
To wreck the ship and send her crew
Past hope of saving neath the waves
To Davy Jones and wat'ry graves!

(Laughs fiendishly and exits L. LIGHTS UP.
Open traverse tabs; swing cloth from side to side.
Enter SARAH R., carrying a sheet and a pencil.)

SARAH      Tommy! Tommy! Puss, puss, puss, puss! Oh, where has he got to? (Stops C. and sways in opposite direction to cloth, as with the motion of a ship.) Ooh, I do wish the floor would keep still on this ship. (Cloth stops.) Ah, that's better -- I've found me sea legs. Now I can get on with me sewing. The Captain's sent me below to mend the mainsail, because the Mate's put his toe through it again. I'm very worried about Tommy, though. We haven't been able to find him ever since the ship started. Ooh, I've had an idea. I'll get all of you to help me to find him. I'm sure if we make a lot of noise he's bound to hear us, so let's sing a song together. The only thing is, I haven't a song handy. Never mind, I'll write one. Er - (Thinks a moment.) Ah! (Writes about one word on sheet, then opens it to display printed words of song-sheet.)
There, didn't take long, did it? And just by chance, there's a convenient batten here for me to hang it on so you can all see it. (Turns U.S.)
I said there's a convenient batten here.
(Batten drops from flies.) Thank you.
(Hangs sheet on batten.)

|          | Now I'm sure –   (Conductor's name.)   can find us a bit of a tune to fit it, can't you? |
|----------|---|
| CONDUCTOR | Yes, of course, Sarah. |
| SARAH    | Ah, I thought you'd say that. Well, you play it over then, so I can teach the others. |

(MUSIC 39   'CATAWAUL')

Ev'ry little kitten goes squeak, squeak, squeak,
   So quietly you often wonder how!
     Then you hear a growing 'Purr',
     From the middle of its fur.
   And it ends up with a huge 'MEOW'.

(SARAH now gets Audience to sing, stressing the need for plenty of volume so that TOMMY will hear. After a suitable number of times:)
Magnificent! Oh, I'm sure Tommy must have heard that.

|          |   |
|----------|---|
| TOMMY    | (at back of auditorium, unseen by Audience) MEOW! |
| SARAH    | Wait a minute, what's that? |
|          | (HOUSELIGHTS UP.) |
| TOMMY    | (coming into auditorium)   MEOW! |
| SARAH    | It's Tommy! We have found him! |
| TOMMY    | (moves towards stage, making friends with some of children) |
| SARAH    | Would you like to bring some of those children up here, Tommy? |
| TOMMY    | (indicates emphatically that he would) |
| SARAH    | Well, come along then.   (Ad-lib with children coming up on stage, singing song and returning to auditorium.)   Oh, that was very good, wasn't it, Tommy? |
| TOMMY    | (heartily agrees) |
| SARAH    | And I'm so glad they found you. By the way, where have you been? |
| TOMMY    | (whispers confidentially in her ear) |

2 – 7 – 75

| | |
|---|---|
| SARAH | Oh, I see. Yes - well - I'm sorry I asked, dear. (Looks in amazement at Audience.) He's been up in the crow's nest looking for crows. Now, before we go, Tommy, shall we let them sing just once more? |
| TOMMY | (nods) |
| SARAH | Right then, last time, so really let yourselves go. |

(As the song is sung for the last time fly song sheet. Close traverse tabs and fly out cloth. SARAH and TOMMY wave goodbye to Audience and exit.)

BLACKOUT

(Open traverse tabs.)

PART II

Scene Eight - THE MAIN DECK OF THE 'SAUCY SAL'

(Full set. Rostrum representing poop deck at stern of ship, with cut-out of stern bulwarks along back of rostrum. Ship's wheel C. of rostrum, with a small hooter attached to it. Line and sinker set at back of rostrum. Telescope set on brackets at back of rostrum. Wings L. and R. showing sail and rigging, etc. 3 mops set in front of wing L. It is night time, moonlight, changing to dawn breaking at end of number. DICK discovered at wheel.

<u>MUSIC 40</u> 'QUIET CONTENT' Words and Music - John Crocker, arranged by Eric Gilder. If feasible, a guitar accompaniment is very suitable for this number.)

DICK          Out at sea, late at night,
                Breeze so cool, moon so bright,
                Waters smooth, ne'er a swell;
                Times like these cast their spell,
                      Bring quiet content.

                Wavelets lap only sound,
                Calms the mind, peace is found,
                Cares are gone, time is still,
                Only such moments will
                      Bring quiet content.

                Workaday toil is done,
                Dreaming time has begun,
                Dreaming time, lazy time,
                Wishing time, hoping time,
                      That's quiet content.

                In the East faint red glow
                Streaks the sky, then doth grow,
                Starlight fades in the dawn,
                All the world is newborn,
                And is content -
                      And is content.

(<u>EFFECT 20.</u> Ship's bell sounds eight bells off. DICK yawns and stretches. <u>MUSIC 41.</u> Hornpipe starts softly and slowly and some CHORUS, as SAILORS, enter dancing wearily to represent the crew just waking up. Music grows louder and quicker and remainder of CHORUS enter dancing a brisker version. Both groups join and are augmented by CAPTAIN, MATE, JACK, in sailor's costume, TOMMY, in sailor's cap; and finally SARAH in WRNS uniform. Dance gets faster and wilder and ends with everyone in a muddled heap. SARAH, supported by JACK and MATE, exits D.L. TOMMY joins DICK at wheel and CAPTAIN moves up to rostrum.)

**CAPTAIN** Good morning, me hearties.

**ALL** (saluting) Good morning, Captain.

**CAPTAIN** And a find morning it is, eh, Mr Mate? (Claps DICK heartily on back, making him lurch forward.)

**DICK** Oh, yes, a splendid morning, Captain.

(Claps CAPTAIN on back even more heartily and knocks him over. TOMMY finds fishing rod and starts to fish.)

**CAPTAIN** Oh, you are rough. (Rises.)

**DICK** I say, I'm awfully sorry.

**CAPTAIN** Never mind, we sailors have to be tough, you know, shiver me timbers.

**DICK** Yes, I suppose we do, er - shake me reef knots.

**CAPTAIN** Ah, I see you're picking up the naval lingo, splice me sidebooms.

**DICK** Well, just an odd phrase here and there, er - splay me seaboots.

**CAPTAIN** Yes. The trouble is, you run out of expressions after a bit, don't you, er - biff me bulkheads?

**DICK** You certainly do, er - er - batter me bilgepipes.

**CAPTAIN** Yes, well, er - um - bust me barnacles, I think you'd better take these hands for'ard and swill the scuppers. (Takes over wheel.) And while you're swilling the scuppers you can swill the skaucers, too.

**DICK** (salutes) Aye, aye, Cap'n. Come along, lads.

|   |   |
|---|---|
|  | (All salute and exit R.) |
| CAPTAIN | (to TOMMY) Mr Second and a half, you can stop fishing and take over mousing duties in the galley. |
| TOMMY | (salutes smartly and eagerly scampers off D.L.) |
| CAPTAIN | Now, where's my working party? (Calling to L.) Working party, ahoy! |
| MATE | (off L.) Just coming. (Entering U.L. and calling off.) Heave! Heave! |
|  | (Enter JACK and SARAH L. pulling on a rope. MATE stops U.S. of rope in C. as they continue hauling across the stage and off R.) |
|  | Heave! Heave! |
| CAPTAIN | What are they doing? |
| MATE | Hauling up the working party. (Calling to R. after them.) Heave! Heave! |
| CAPTAIN | (looking off R.) But I thought they were the working party. |
|  | (Enter JACK and SARAH U.L., holding end of rope.) |
| JACK, SARAH | That's right, we are. (They throw rope off R.) |
| SARAH | What do you want us to do, Captain? |
| CAPTAIN | Well, as you're the working party you can come up here. |
|  | (JACK and SARAH go up R.C. steps onto rostrum.) |
|  | And do some work. |
| JACK | Oh, well in that case, I've just remembered something else I've got to go and do. |
| CAPTAIN | What's that? |
| JACK | Sleep. (Falls asleep. Audience shout. JACK wakes.) Oh, ta. You see, I must go and have a little nap. (Turns to move down steps again.) |
| CAPTAIN | Oh no, you don't, my lad. (Catches hold of waist of JACK's trousers, which is on elastic and very large so that it stretches out.) |

|  |  |
|---|---|
|  | Here, you're supposed to have bell bottoms, not bell tops. |
| JACK | Well, these started life as a bell tent. |
|  | (CAPTAIN releases waistband so that it snaps back.) |
| MATE | Oh, I like that. Can I have a go? |
| JACK | (hastily moving away)   No. |
|  | (But MATE grabs waistband and releases it sharply.) |
|  | Ow! |
| SARAH | My turn! |
|  | (Grabs for waistband but misses it as JACK runs down L.C. steps. She pursues him and catches hold of band just as he is running up R.C. steps so that she pulls trousers down revealing long-legged pants. Music whizz as she does so. Hiding her face.) |
|  | Ooh! |
| JACK | There, now look what you've done. |
| SARAH | I daren't. |
| JACK | (hurriedly pulling trousers up)   I'll probably catch a cold in me coms now. |
| CAPTAIN | Come here, you two, I want to give you some instruction in seamanship. |
|  | (JACK and SARAH move onto rostrum.) |
|  | Mr Mate, take the wheel. |
| MATE | What for? I don't want it. |
| CAPTAIN | Do as I tell you, Wilfrid, and take the wheel. |
| MATE | Oh, all right.   (Picks up wheel and moves away with it.)   Where shall I take it to? |
| CAPTAIN | Put it back! |
| MATE | But you just told me to take it. |
| CAPTAIN | I know. You have to take it where it is. |
| MATE | How can I take it where it is? It's there already. |

| | |
|---|---|
| CAPTAIN | Just stand behind it and twiddle it. |
| | (MATE 'twiddles' wheel.) |
| | Not over there - over here! |
| MATE | We-ll, seems a waste of time to me. (Replaces wheel and stands behind it.) |
| | (EFFECT 21. Ship's bell sounds four bells off.) |
| SARAH | I say. |
| CAPTAIN | Yes? |
| SARAH | I think there's somebody at the front door. |
| CAPTAIN | Don't be silly. We don't have front doors on ships. That bell's what we tell the time by. |
| JACK | Tell the time by? |
| CAPTAIN | Yes, it's just sounded four bells. |
| MATE | (takes out a small bell on a chain from pocket and looks at it) It's slow then. I make it ten tinkles past. |
| CAPTAIN | Well, your bell always gives the wrong chime. |
| MATE, JACK, SARAH | Ooh! |
| | (MATE puts bell away.) |
| CAPTAIN | Now then, I'm going to teach you two how to keep a lookout. (Points L.) Look, there's the port. |
| SARAH | Oh, goody. I'd love a glass. |
| CAPTAIN | I mean, there's the port bow. |
| | (JACK and SARAH look a little mystified, but bow to L.) |
| CAPTAIN | (pointing R.) And there's the starboard. |
| SARAH and JACK | Bow? |
| CAPTAIN | Bow. |
| | (JACK and SARAH bow to R. CAPTAIN takes telescope from brackets. It has a T.V. aerial on the front of it.) |

And this - this is the telescope.

JACK
(pointing to aerial) What's that for?

CAPTAIN
To show it's a 'tele' - scope, of course. On a clear day you can get I.T.V. and B.B.C. Now you look through it and tell me what you see.

SARAH
Righto. (Looks off L., extending telescope so that a flexible piece comes out and bends towards her toes.)

CAPTAIN
What can you see?

SARAH
Me feet.

CAPTAIN
What! Now look what you've done, ruined my lovely telescope. (Takes it and replaces it on brackets.)

MATE
I say, does this wheel do anything?

CAPTAIN
Of course it does, it works the rudder.

MATE
I don't think it does.

CAPTAIN
Oh, and why not?

MATE
'Cos the rudder came off just after we started.

CAPTAIN
What? I thought you said you'd fixed it nice and firm.

MATE
So I did. I tied it with two knots and a bow, but I don't think that pink ribbon was strong enough.

CAPTAIN
Oh, you are a rotten sailor, really you are. Well, you can stop twiddling that wheel then. We'll have some deck cleaning drill instead. Party - get your mops.

(They run U.L. and get a mop each.)

SARAH
(holding her mop next to JACK's) Which twin has the Toni?

CAPTAIN
Now then, now then, you're on parade.

(They line up facing R., MATE first, JACK second, and SARAH third, holding their mops heads upwards in their L. hands.)

CAPTAIN
Party - 'shun!

(They come to attention very smartly.)

(Rather taken aback by their smartness.) Ooh. Party - shoulder mops!

(They put mops on their L. shoulders. MATE's goes into JACK's face and JACK's into SARAH's face. JACK and SARAH make elaborate business of removing pieces of mop from their mouths.)

Get back in line there!

(JACK and SARAH obey. SARAH has to lean back at an alarming angle to keep out of the way of JACK's mop.)

Party - quick march!

(They march to C., SARAH having difficulty in catching up with step, and collide with CAPTAIN, who doesn't halt them soon enough, so that they keep marking time, JACK with MATE's mop in his face and SARAH with JACK's.)

Party - halt! HALT!

(They halt and JACK and SARAH again remove pieces of mop from their mouths.)

Get back in line at once!

(They do so.)

Party - left turn!

(They turn L. MATE's mop knocks over JACK and JACK's SARAH. CAPTAIN moves to L. of SARAH as she hastily pulls down her skirt which has allowed her bloomers to show.)

Now then, now then! Such immodesty. On your tootsies immediately.

(JACK and SARAH rise.)

Get your dressing.

(JACK and SARAH very exaggeratedly dress on MATE, ending with SARAH stamping out - pom-tiddley-om-pom and JACK -pom-pom.)

Party - down mops!

|  |  |
|---|---|
|  | (They bring down their mops, MATE's onto JACK's foot, JACK's onto SARAH's foot and SARAH's onto CAPTAIN's foot.) |
| JACK, SARAH and CAPTAIN | (hopping round holding their feet)   OW! |
| CAPTAIN | (to SARAH)   Do be more careful. |
| SARAH | (to JACK)   Do be more careful. |
| JACK | (to MATE)   -Do be more careful. |
| MATE | (turning to R.)   Do be - oh.   (Realising that there is nobody hits own R. foot with mop.) OW!   (Hopping round on good foot.)   Now look what you've made me do.   (Throws mop down.) I'm sick of being a sailor. |
| SARAH | (throwing her mop aside and buffeting CAPTAIN in rear as she does so)   So am I. |
| JACK | (throws his mop away)   And me. |
| CAPTAIN | Well, with a crew like you I'd sooner be ashore meself. |
| SARAH, JACK and MATE | Let's turn round and go back. |
|  | (MUSIC 42 'WE WISH WE HADN'T GONE TO SEA' Words by John Crocker, Music by Eric Gilder.) |
|  | We wish we hadn't gone to sea, We wish we'd stay'd at home; We're sick of the sight of water, Sick of the briny foam. |
| MATE | I'd like to be a porter, slamming doors, you see, Wham! Biff! Bangity-wallop! That's the job for me. |
| ALL | We wish we hadn't, etc. |
| CAPTAIN | I'd like to be a fishmonger, selling fish for tea, Plaice! Dace! Cockle and scallop! |
| MATE | Wham! Biff! etc. |
| CAP and MATE | That's the job for we. |
| ALL | We wish we hadn't, etc. |

| | |
|---|---|
| SARAH | I'd like to be a painter, slapping on paint so free, Splish! Splosh! Dribble and dollop! |
| CAPTAIN | Plaice! Dace! etc. |
| MATE | Wham! Biff! etc. |
| ALL 3 | That's the job for we. |
| ALL | We wish we hadn't, etc. |
| JACK | I'd like to be a horseman, all day in the saddle I'd be, Clip, clop, canter and – (Stops, thinking. OTHERS look at him.) gollop! |
| SARAH | Splish! Splosh! etc. |
| CAPTAIN | Plaice! Dace! etc. |
| MATE | Wham! Biff! etc. |
| ALL | That's the job for we. (Very, very fast.) We wish we hadn't gone to sea, We wish we'd stay'd at home; We're sick of the sight of water, Sick of the briny foam. And now we've told you all the things that we would like to be. Clip, clop, canter and gollop! Splish! Splosh! Dribble and dollop! Plaice! Dace! Cockle and scallop! Wham! Biff! Bangity-wallop! They're the jobs for we! |
| VOICE | (off R.) Land ahoy! (Enter DICK R.) |
| DICK | Captain, there's a rocky coast off our starboard bow. |
| SARAH | Ah, Dover, no doubt. |
| DICK | And there's a storm brewing. |
| CAPTAIN | A storm? Is the glass falling? |

(EFFECT 22. Glass crash off R.)

| | |
|---|---|
| JACK, SARAH | Yes. (They move onto rostrum, SARAH to wheel.) |
| CAPTAIN | Mr Mates, call all hands on deck. |
| DICK and MATE | (saluting) Aye, aye, Cap'n. (DICK calls to R., MATE to L.) All hands on deck! All hands on deck! |
| | (TOMMY enters R. and joins DICK. CHORUS enter L. and R.) |
| CAPTAIN | Clear the decks, lads, and stand by to batten the hatches and reef the foretops. |
| CHORUS | Aye, aye, aye, Cap'n. (They clear away the mops.) |
| CAPTAIN | (looking off R.) We're running in too close to that rocky coast. (To SARAH.) Give a blast on the ship's siren. |
| SARAH | Certainly. (Toots hooter attached to wheel.) |
| CAPTAIN | Hm, most inadequate. We'll have to take soundings. (To JACK.) Get the line and sinker. |
| JACK | Sink what? The ship? |
| CAPTAIN | No, no, no. (Picks up weighted line from back of rostrum.) This thing here. This is the line and this is the sinker. Throw it over and sound the depth. |
| JACK | (takes it) Oh. Throw it over – (Moves hand back with weight to do so and hits CAPTAIN on head.) |
| CAPTAIN | (dancing round rubbing head) OW! |
| JACK | (throwing weight over the stern) And sound the depth. (Leans over with a hand cupped to ear.) Can't hear a thing. (Straightening up and gripping line.) I've got a bite, though! |
| | (The line plays out.) |
| | Quick, help! |

|         | (SARAH and MATE get behind him on line.) |
|---------|------------------------------------------|
| MATE    | Ooh, it's a whopper! |
| JACK    | Maybe it's a shark! |
| SARAH   | Feels more like a whale! |
| ALL 3   | (they are nearly pulled over back)   Oops! |
| CAPTAIN | (getting behind them on line)   Lend a hand there! |
| DICK    | Come on, lads! |
|         | (DICK jumps to help with line, CHORUS get behind him and TOMMY gets on end.) |
| CAPTAIN | Now then, heave ho, me hearties! |
| DICK    | Heave, lads! Heave! Heave! |
| SARAH   | Do stop shouting heave! You're making me feel ill again. |
| JACK    | Here it comes! |
|         | (All move back, GREEN FLASH C. <u>MUSIC 43.</u> KING RAT appears holding end of line. GREEN SPOT on to him, BLACKOUT everything else. LIGHTNING FLASHES, <u>EFFECT 23.</u> Thunder. FADE UP LIGHTS for storm atmosphere.) |
| KING RAT | Aha!<br>Ye mortal fools, ye all are doom'd,<br>Soon neath the waves ye'll lie entomb'd! |
|         | (DICK, TOMMY and CHORUS have jumped away from rope. CAPTAIN, MATE, JACK and SARAH have fallen over.) |
| DICK    | Who's this? |
| SARAH   | I'd sooner not be told;<br>He looks like rather nasty mould. |
| JACK    | It's Ratty! |
| MATE    | Help! |
| CAPTAIN | Get off my ship! |
| KING RAT | Thou dolt! I hold thee in my grip.<br>Come ye, my storm sprites, to my call, |

Stir up the mighty waters all!
Make thunder roar with cannon crash!

(EFFECT 24. Thunder.)

And lightning strike in blinding flash!

(LIGHTNING.)

Rouse up the gale winds from their sleep!

(EFFECT 25. Wind noise.)

And cast this ship into the deep!

(ALL run to and fro in great panic as storm effects build up.)

CAPTAIN We've struck! Abandon ship! Abandon ship!

(Screams, shouts, more panic, some take up CAPTAIN's cry, demonic laughter from KING RAT and:)

BLACKOUT

(Close traverse tabs. Fly in Scene 9 frontcloth, if used. MUSIC 44.)

## PART II

### Scene Nine - THE SHORES OF MOROCCO

(Tabs to begin opening as soon as convenient during scene to reveal frontcloth representing sandy shore with coconut palm painted C. If a cloth is impractical, open tabs to reveal a 6 ft. flat similarly painted. Enter DICK R.)

DICK — I wonder where I am? Well, at least it's dry land. I seem to be the only one saved from the wreck. All the others must have been drowned - and Tommy with them, I'm afraid. Oh, if only I could have saved him. (Sighs.) Poor Tommy.

(Enter TOMMY R.)

I shall miss him dreadfully.

TOMMY — (sees DICK and 'Meows' loudly and joyfully)

DICK — There now, I'm imagining I can hear him.

TOMMY — MEOW!

DICK — Or am I? (Turns.) Tommy!

(They run and greet each other effusively.)

How did you save yourself?

TOMMY — (motion diving and swimming)

DICK — I didn't know you could swim. I though you hated water.

TOMMY — (nods emphatically, which reminds him of water in his ear, waggles R. paw in R. ear, shakes his head to R., at the same time banging L. side of head with L. paw. Jet of water squirts from ear)

DICK — (laughs) Never mind, Tommy. Let's do some exploring and see if this place is inhabited. We must find some food, too. I wonder where though? Let's think. (Assumes a thinking posture, head in hand, elbow supported by other hand.)

TOMMY — (copies DICK's thinking posture. Is suddenly struck by a brilliant idea and runs off R.)

DICK — Tommy, where are you going? Hey, Tommy!

(EFFECT 26. Sound of big splash off R.)

| | |
|---|---|
| DICK | TOMMY! |
| TOMMY | (returns, very pleased with himself, holding large fish in mouth, which he places at DICK's feet) |
| DICK | (picking up fish)   Tommy, you're brilliant. |
| TOMMY | (modestly agrees, then finds he has water in his ear again and deals with it as before) |
| DICK | I say, it's a whopper. Let's see if we can find something to make a fire and cook it. |

(They exit L. Slight pause and CAPTAIN enters R. very bedraggled.)

| | |
|---|---|
| CAPTAIN | I'm the only one saved from the wreck. Me lovely ship's sunk and here I am all by meself on a desert island. |

(MATE staggers on R. also very bedraggled, with his mouth blown out.)

Wilfrid! Oh, Wilfrid, am I glad to see you. Wilfrid, speak to me, Wilfrid.

| | |
|---|---|
| MATE | (squirting CAPTAIN with the water his mouth is filled with)   Hullo. |
| CAPTAIN | Look out! I've had enough of water for the present. What we need now is some food. (Looks round.)   There we are, everything laid on, coconuts. Climb on my shoulders and reach 'em down. |
| MATE | All right. |

(They move underneath palm and MATE tries to stretch his legs sufficiently to step onto CAPTAIN's shoulders.)

I say.

| | |
|---|---|
| CAPTAIN | Yes? |
| MATE | You haven't got a lower pair of shoulders, have you? |
| CAPTAIN | Don't be silly. But I tell you what, I'll sit down. |

|  |  |
|---|---|
|  | (Sits and MATE gingerly climbs onto his shoulders, and in a rather crouched position, holding onto CAPTAIN's hair with one hand, reaches up with other.) |
| MATE | It's no good. I can't reach. |
| CAPTAIN | Hang on then. I'll stand up. |
| MATE | No, don't do that, I don't like heights. |
| CAPTAIN | Don't be silly, they're just the same as lows only further up.     (Starts to rise.) |
| MATE | Ooh! I'm going to fall! I'm going to fall! (Grasps CAPTAIN's hair with both hands.) |
| CAPTAIN | Here, mind my hair. And don't wobble about so much! |
| MATE | It's not me, it's you that's wobbling. Aah! Look out! |
|  | (Falls forward onto CAPTAIN who falls backwards.) |
| CAPTAIN | (speaking with difficulty)    Take your foot out of me mouth! |
|  | (They disentangle themselves and rise.) |
|  | Fine coconut picker you turned out to be. |
| MATE | It's not my fault. We chose the wrong tree. Let's see if we can find a little one - the same size as they have at fairs. |
| CAPTAIN | What do you mean - the same size as they have at fairs? |
| MATE | You know, at the coconut shies they grow little coconut trees about this high.    (Indicates with hand.) |
| CAPTAIN | Oh yes. But we'll have to find one of those little boxes that grow beside 'em first, though. |
| MATE | Why? |
| CAPTAIN | 'Cos in the little boxes grow the little wooden balls to knock 'em down with. |
|  | (They exit L. Slight pause. Enter SARAH R., |

dressed in her underwear, carrying a large bag.)

SARAH  I'm the only one saved from the wreck; and somewhere or other there's a shark swimming round the ocean in a Wren's uniform - I slipped out at one end as he came for me at the other.   (Diving into bag.)   Never mind, fortunately I happened to bring me knitting needles with me, so I'll be able to run up a grass skirt in no time.   (Brings out large knitting needles.  Moves round looking at backcloth.)   Oh dear, oh dear, there doesn't seem to be any grass here.   (Diving into bag.) Never mind, fortunately I happened to bring some grass seed with me.   (Brings out large packet of grass seed.)   Now, I'll plant it.   (Moves round looking at backcloth.)   Oh dear, oh <u>dear</u> - there doesn't seem to be any earth here either. (Diving into bag.)   Never mind, fortunately I happened to bring some earth with me.   (Brings out large flowerpot.)   I'll pop them in . (Scatters some seeds from packet into pot.) There, they won't be long.   (Hums to self for a few seconds holding pot then looks inside.) Not ready.  What a pity I didn't happen to bring my desert island discs to play while I'm waiting. (Continues humming then looks again.)   Ah, ready!   (Pulls skein of raffia from pot.) Now, cast on.   (Fits raffia onto needles. Moving L. speaking rhythmically.)   And knit one, purl one, knit one, purl one, knit one, purl one, knit one, drop one - pickit up,   (Does so.) and purl one, knit one, purl one, knit one, (Disappears L.)   purl one, knit one, purl one - cast off.   (Re-enters wearing grass skirt.) That's better.  Now I must have something to eat. Oh, how handy, a coconut tree.  Excuse me, while I run up and get a coconut.   (Tries to shin up tree and falls down.)   Ooh, what a slippery tree.   (Putting things back in bag.)   Never mind, I'll explore a little and I daresay I'll come across a Wimpy Bar.   (Or well-know local cafe. Exit L.)

(Slight pause.  Enter JACK R. in old-fashioned

long-legged, striped bathing costume.)

JACK    I'm the only one saved from the wreck. In fact, I've brought the wreck with me. (Holds up a porthole labelled 'Saucy Sal' and puts his head through it.) There, that's all that's left of the 'Saucy Sal', one porthole. Still, it feels good to have a bit of solid under me feet again. I wish I'd got a bit of solid in me tummy too. (Looks round.) Ah, a coconut palm. Well, if I throw the 'Saucy Sal' up at it I might be able to knock one down. (Tries.) And then again, I might not. (Tries a couple more throws and turns away disappointed.) No, and I used to be jolly good at knocking down conkers.

(MUSIC whizz as prop coconut falls on his head thrown on from as high as possible offstage, and he is knocked out by it. Slight pause. <u>MUSIC 45.</u> Enter PRINCESS ULUL L.)

ULUL    Ooh. A man. How nice. I wake. (Shakes JACK.) Nice man. Wake up. (Shakes him again.) Me nice girl. Worth waking for.

(JACK comes round. ULUL cuddles him in her arms.)

JACK    What? Where am I? What happened? (Looks at ULUL in astonishment.) I think I must be dreaming.

ULUL    Me Ulul.

JACK    You what-what?

ULUL    Ulul. Should be Lulu, but this very backward country. Who you-you?

JACK    Oh, me Jack-Jack.

ULUL    Jack-Jack. I like-like.

JACK    Me, too-too.

ULUL    No, you Jack-Jack. Me Princess Ulul.

JACK    A princess? There, I said I was dreaming.

ULUL    Me Princess - daughter Emperor of Occorom.

| | |
|---|---|
| JACK | Occorom? Where's Occorom? |
| ULUL | Morocco. I tell you this very backward country. |
| JACK | Well, If I am dreaming, I might as well make the most of such a pretty dream while it lasts. (Kisses her.) |
| ULUL | You like?   (Kisses him back.) |
| JACK | Yes, me do like.   (Kisses her again.)   Me like very much.   (Kisses her arm from finger-tips to shoulder.)   Ah, coffee flavour. You know, these kisses seem very real. Maybe it's not a dream, after all. I'd better make sure.<br><br>(He attempts to kiss her again but she moves away to R.) |
| ULUL | No more-more. Not now-now. Papa waiting. Me go-go. 'Bye-bye, Jack-Jack. |
| JACK | Oh, no-no. Don't go-go.   (Runs after her.) |
| ULUL | (slipping past him to L.)   Oh, yes-yes. Me must-must. |
| JACK | (catching her hand)   Well, just give me one more kiss-kiss before I wake up. |
| ULUL | All right-right. |
| JACK | I'll have it - just there.   (Points with finger to C. of L. cheek.) |
| ULUL | One kiss-kiss.<br><br>(JACK closes eyes and ecstatically makes a funny appreciative noise as she kisses him.)<br><br>Now bye-bye.   (Runs off L.) |
| JACK | No, before bye-bye, one more-more.<br><br>(Turns to kiss her but grasps instead SARAH, who has just entered backwards from L. He opens his eyes and realises his mistake just before imparting a kiss.)<br><br>Ooh! Ugh-ugh! Now I'm having nightmares. |
| SARAH | Jack! I thought you were drowndeded. |

| | |
|---|---|
| JACK | No, me-me swim-swim – I mean, swum-swum. |
| SARAH | Swam? |
| JACK | S'right. |
| BOTH | Then we're the only two saved from the wreck. |
| | (Enter CAPTAIN backwards L., shaking head at MATE who is following and bumps into SARAH.) |
| SARAH | (turning)   Here, who are you a-shoving-of – Captain Cuttle! |
| JACK | Mr Scuttle! |
| CAP and MATE | Sarah and Jack! |
| SARAH | I wonder if there's any more of us anywhere? |
| | (Enter TOMMY L.) |
| TOMMY | Meow! |
| ALL | Tommy! |
| SARAH | Oh, what a pity your poor master wasn't saved. |
| DICK | (entering L.)   But I was! |
| ALL | Dick!   (All greet him.) |
| DICK | Well, isn't this wonderful, here we all are, safe and sound. |
| | (4 CHORUS enter L. as CASSIM, Captain of the Moroccan Guard, and guardsmen ALI, ABDUL and FAKRASH. CASSIM has scimitar, others carry spears.) |
| CASSIM | Strangers!  Seize them! |
| | (GUARDS surround others, threatening them with spears. FAKRASH takes fish from DICK. TOMMY leaps away to R.C. and stands arching back, snarling and spitting.) |
| SARAH | Here, what's this lot? |
| MATE | Hey, what's going on? |
| CAPTAIN | Where did these blokes pop up from? |

– (Together as they are surrounded.)

| | |
|---|---|
| JACK | What's happening? |
| DICK | Don't you threaten me! |
| SARAH | You can't treat me like this. |

(CASSIM jabs her in rear with scimitar.)

Ow! I was wrong. You can treat me like that.

CASSIM    (pointing to TOMMY) What that?

DICK    That's my cat, and if you hurt –

CASSIM    Cat? Never heard of cat. Abdul, seize cat!

(ABDUL advances on TOMMY rather nervously. TOMMY backs slowly. ABDUL lunges out, TOMMY swiftly jumps aside and bites ABDUL's leg, then turns and runs off R.)

ABDUL    (hopping round holding leg) OW!

CASSIM    Leave cat. Take prisoners to Emperor. March!

(Close traverse tabs. Fly out cloth. PRISONERS move L., SARAH brings up rear.)

SARAH    Oh, I say, we're going to be presented.

(CASSIM pokes SARAH with scimitar.)

Ow! I get your point.

**BLACKOUT**

(<u>MUSIC 46.</u> Open traverse tabs.)

PART II

Scene Ten - THE EMPEROR OF MOROCCO'S
PALACE

(Full set. Moorish decor. Cut-out ground-row of pillared balcony along front of rostrum. Steps down C., in front of rostrum. Wings L. and R. L.C. a dais, overhung with a canopy and piled with cushions. EMPEROR OF MOROCCO, very dark-skinned and much be-turbanned, discovered seated on the pile of cushions smoking a hookah and watching some of CHORUS as his WIVES, dressed in Eastern costume with yashmaks, etc., dancing Oriental Dance, led by ULUL. One of CHORUS stands behind EMPEROR as his attendant MUSTAPHA, fanning him with a punkah. Dance ends with all bowing low to EMPEROR.)

EMPEROR (speaks with very posh accent) Oh, jolly good show. Thank you, wifeys. And daughter, too, of course. (Draws on hookah and splutters.) Ugh! Disgusting!

(WIVES bow low again and retire to R. ULUL joins her father.)

ULUL Papa no like?

EMPEROR No, can't think why I smoke the wretched thing. But one must do something to pass the time. Can hardly even eat nowadays with all these beastly rats overrunning the country. I suppose I might make the food go a bit further by executing the wifeys, but - well, they do come in useful sometimes.

ULUL Papa must not execute my mummies. Not nice.

EMPEROR Oh, I don't know. An execution or two does pass the time. (Yawns.)

(Enter CASSIM R. on rostrum, moves to EMPEROR and grovels before him, bowing head to ground with hands outstretched.)

CASSIM Majesty.

EMPEROR What is it, Cassim, old man? Got a pain?

CASSIM (rises) Majesty, me capture five strangers.

EMPEROR Oh, well done, Cassim. Bring 'em in and let's

|  |  |
|---|---|
|  | have a dekko at 'em. |
| CASSIM | Yes, Majesty.   (Bows then calls off R.) Bring in prisoners. |
|  | (ALI, ABDUL and FAKRASH march on DICK, CAPTAIN, MATE, JACK and SARAH.) |
| SARAH | (as they enter)   Ooh, I say, isn't it posh? |
|  | (ALI pokes her in rear with spear.) |
|  | Ow! Here, Jack, change places. |
| JACK | All right. |
|  | (They change places. ALI jabs JACK with spear.) |
|  | Ow! |
| ULUL | Jack-Jack! |
| JACK | (stepping forward)   Ulul! |
|  | (ALI prods him again.) |
|  | Ow!   (Steps back.)   Stop it! You'll puncture me in a minute. |
| CASSIM | (raising scimitar threateningly)   Silence! Grovel before the Emperor. |
| SARAH | Ooh, royalty! I'm all of a doodah! |
| CASSIM | Grovel! |
|  | (SARAH curtsies, losing balance, CAPTAIN and MATE salute, DICK nods curtly and JACK waves familiarly to EMPEROR.) |
| JACK | Hullo, Emp-Emp.   (To others.)   You'd better leave this to me - I've learnt the language. (To EMPEROR.)   Now listen carefully, Emp-Emp. Me Jack-Jack, this Sar-Sar, Mate-Mate, Cap-Cap and Dick-Dick. We shipwrecked. You twig-twig? |
| EMPEROR | Oh, yes-yes. Like anything, old chap-chap. I'm an absolute dab-dab at translating pidgin. |
| CAPTAIN | (to JACK)   What do you mean, you speak the language? |

| | |
|---|---|
| MATE | Old Emp-Emp speaks English just as well as what we do. |
| EMPEROR | Better, my dear Mate-Mate, better. Jolly bad luck your ship getting pranged, still I'm very glad you were all spared a watery grave. I'm sure you'll much prefer being executed. |
| PRISONERS | Much - Executed?! |
| EMPEROR | Yes. I know it must seem terribly inhospitable, but we're so terribly short of food here due to a plague of rats, that I'm having to keep the population down to an absolute minimum. But I'll make it as comfortable for you as possible. Mustapha, go and get out the plush-padded block. |
| MUSTAPHA | Yes, Majesty. (Bows, hitting EMPEROR on head with punkah.) |
| EMPEROR | (rubbing head) And tell them to use it on you first. |
| | (Exit MUSTAPHA L.) |
| | Well, jolly nice to have met you all. Sorry we have to part so soon. (Claps hands.) Guards! |
| | (GUARDS hustle them to R.) |
| JACK | But I know your daughter! |
| MATE | But I don't want to be executed - not on a Tuesday! |
| CAPTAIN | But you can't execute me - I've got a dirty neck! |
| SARAH | But I've never been executed before - I don't know whether I'll like it! |
| DICK | Wait! <u>Wait!</u> |
| | (Manages to break free from GUARDS.) Your Majesty, I've just thought, we can give you some food. My cat caught a great big fish. |
| EMPEROR | Your what did you say caught a fish? |
| DICK | My cat. |

(Over-lapping) — applies to JACK, MATE, CAPTAIN, SARAH, DICK lines above.

| | |
|---|---|
| EMPEROR | Cat? What's a cat? |
| CASSIM | Cat – huge!  (Puts hand above head to indicate height.) |
| FAKRASH | Fierce! |
| ALI | Terrible! |
| ABDUL | (rubbing leg)  Bites. |
| EMPEROR | Well, we'll go into that later. The fish is the important thing at the moment. Where is it? |
| DICK | One of your guards took it from me. |
| | (FAKRASH starts sneaking off R.) |
| EMPEROR | Fakrash! |
| | (FAKRASH stops.) |
| | Bad luck, Fakrash, you nearly got away with it. Let's have the fish, Fakrash. |
| | (FAKRASH sorrowfully takes fish from inside coat and gives it to EMPEROR.) |
| | Thanks, dear lad. Now be a good chap and run along and get yourself executed, Fakrash. |
| FAKRASH | Yes, Majesty.  (Bows and exits dejectedly R.) |
| EMPEROR | Amusing bloke, old Fakrash. Sometimes I have to execute him two or three times a week. Well, this must be cooked at once, I'm absolutely starving. Ulul, wifeys! |
| ULUL | Yes, Papa?       (Together.) |
| WIVES | Yes, husband? |
| EMPEROR | Pop this into a pan, dears, and serve it up as soon as possible. |
| ULUL | (taking fish)  Yes, Papa.     (Together.) |
| WIVES | Yes, husband. |
| | (They bow and exit L.) |
| EMPEROR | Now this cat thing you were talking about. Is it really so huge and fierce? |

| | |
|---|---|
| DICK | No, your Majesty, but it is a very valuable animal. It's natural enemies are rats. |
| EMPEROR | Really? |
| DICK | My cat, Sire, would deal with your plague of rats in a twinkling. |
| EMPEROR | Sounds just the ticket. Where is it? |
| DICK | Unfortunately your Majesty's guards attacked it and forced it to flee when we were taken prisoner. |
| EMPEROR | Oh, I say, Cassim, you and the boys have boobed. |
| | (CASSIM nods shamefacedly.) |
| | Makes me look a ripe Charlie. Well, pop out now and recover this valuable animal. |
| CASSIM | Yes, Majesty.   (Bows.)   Guards. |
| | (They start to go out R.) |
| EMPEROR | Oh, and Cassim. |
| CASSIM | (stopping)   Majesty? |
| EMPEROR | When you and the boys get back, run along and get executed. |
| CASSIM | (sighs)   Yes, Majesty. |
| | (He exits with ABDUL and ALI.) |
| EMPEROR | Funny thing is, every time I execute them they turn up again. Most odd. Well, this cat of yours may persuade me to change my mind about executing you. Might keep you on as court entertainers or something. Can you do anything in that line? |
| | (They look at each other glumly, then SARAH is struck with an idea and dives into her bag.) |
| SARAH | Yes! Fortunately, I happened to bring some music with me.   (Brings out sheets of music.) |
| CAPTAIN | Oh well, if you're going to sing that settles it. (To EMPEROR.)   Which way is the execution block? |
| SARAH | No, no, no. We're all going to sing.   (Hands out |

parts to all of them and brings out a knitting needle from bag.) Now listen carefully, Empie, we'll take you on a bit of a spree with a glee. (Moves down to floats and gravely bows to CONDUCTOR. Music starts and she conducts others with a knitting needle.)

(<u>MUSIC 47</u>  'HICKORY DICKORY DOCK'. In the manner of Mozart.)

ALL

Hickory Dickory, Hickory Dickory, Hickory
                Dickory Dock,
  The mouse ran up the clock,
  The mouse ran up the clock,
Hickory Dickory, Hickory Dickory, Hickory
                Dickory Dock.

  The mouse ran up the clock,
  The mouse ran up the clock.
The mouse ran up, the mouse ran up
  Ran up the clock.
The mouse ran up, the mouse ran up
  Ran up the clock.

(Repeat first verse above.)

The clock - struck one.
The clock struck one?
The clock - struck one.
The clock struck one?
The clock struck one, the clock struck one.
The clock struck two,
The clock struck <u>one</u>.
And down the mouse ran,
And down, and down, and down the mouse ran.

Hickory Dickory, Hickory Dickory, Hickory
                Dickory Dock.
  The mouse ran up the clock
  The mouse ran up the clock
Hickory Dickory, Hickory Dickory, Hickory
                Dickory Dock.
  The mouse ran up, the mouse ran up,
    Ran up the clock.
  The mouse ran up, the mouse ran up,
    Ran up the clock.

                    Hickory Dickory Dock
                    The mouse ran up the clock
                    The mouse,
                    The clock,
                    -cory Dick,
                    -cory Dock,
                    -cory Dick,
                    -curried Beef?
                    Dock!
                    Dick!
                    Hick!

EMPEROR         Oh, positively whacko and bang on.

                (Enter ULUL L., preceding a large covered dish,
                wheeled on by WIVES to in from of EMPEROR.)

                Ah, jolly old din-dins.

                (2 WIVES lift cover from dish. GREEN FLASH,
                BLACKOUT, GREEN SPOT UP on KING RAT who
                leaps from platter. MUSIC 48. LIGHTS UP.
                Yells from JACK, SARAH, CAPTAIN and MATE.
                Screams from ULUL and WIVES as remainder of
                CHORUS as RATS run on L. ULUL and WIVES run
                off. JACK jumps into SARAH's arms, MATE into
                CAPTAIN's and they and EMPEROR run round stage
                chased by rats, to exit D.R. RATS remain on.)

KING RAT        (to DICK)
                Ye've 'scap'd me once, ye've 'scap'd me twice,
                I vow ye shall not 'scape me thrice!

                (MUSIC 49. They draw swords and fight until
                DICK is disarmed and KING RAT pinions him to
                pillar with his sword pointing to his heart.)

                Cringe, Whittington, thy day is done!
                Come, minion rats, our vict'ry's won!

                (Steps back, RATS rush to surround DICK, who tries
                to fight them off.)

                Away with him!

                (RATS hustle DICK to R., MUSIC 50 but
                SILVERCHIME appears there and bars their path.)

SILVERCHIME              Hold, rodents vile!

(RATS cower back.)

**KING RAT**     On! On! Let not the sprite beguile!

**SILVERCHIME**     Too late, foul King, thy cause is lost,
And losers aye must pay the cost.
The price for thee is high, King Rat,
For 'tis thy life! Come forth, good cat.

(TOMMY bounds on R. <u>MUSIC 51.</u>)

**KING RAT**     My life? Nay, his! As shall be seen
When sharp rats' teeth his bones pick clean!
On him, ye minions!

(RATS leap at TOMMY, who lays out first one, then another till he has dealt with them all. Slowly he approaches KING RAT.)

Now nothing can thy life defend!
Prepare thee, cat, to meet thy end!

(Throws sword aside and they fling themselves at each other. After a fearsome struggle, in which KING RAT at first seems to have the advantage, TOMMY knocks him sprawling down rostrum steps and leaps on his throat, then stands with one foot on him in triumph.)

**SILVERCHIME**     A triumph! Evil's overthrown!
Once more doth good the vict'ry own!
Brave cat, ye've prov'd a friend most true.

**DICK**     He has, indeed. But - who are you?

**SILVERCHIME**     Thy Fairy Guardian I, good lad.
I've watch'd o'er thee through good and bad,
But now thy life shall happy be;
Henceforth shall fortune smile on thee.
So hie ye swift to London Town,
Where love all other joys shall crown!

(WHITE FLASH. BLACKOUT. Exit SILVERCHIME LIGHTS UP.)

**DICK**     A fairy! Well, I don't know whether to believe my eyes or not. Do you think that really was a fairy, Tommy?

**TOMMY**     (nods emphatically)

(EMPEROR, ULUL and WIVES crowd on from L.)

EMPEROR: Oh, bravo! Jolly good show! I watched the whole thing on closed circuit television. This little fellow's done a magnificent job. The palace is absolutely littered with rats.

(Enter SARAH D.R., carrying JACK pig-a-back.)

SARAH: Is it all over?

(CAPTAIN enters D.R., carrying MATE pig-a-back.)

DICK: Yes, there's nothing to worry about now.

(JACK and MATE get down.)

EMPEROR: Well, now you've saved my kingdom you must be rewarded.

DICK: All I want, your Majesty, is to get back to England.

OTHERS: Hear, hear!

EMPEROR: Simple, my dear fellow, simple. I'll have a ship loaded with riches for you in half a jiffy. Two ships in a quarter of a jiffy if you'll let me keep this game little chappie here.

DICK: Oh no, I couldn't part with Tommy. But why not come with us, Sire, and choose some cats for yourself?

EMPEROR: What a spiffing idea.

ULUL: Me, too-too. Me go with Jack-Jack.

EMPEROR: Certainly. It's high time you learnt to speak properly.

ULUL: Me do speak proper. Proper Occorom.

EMPEROR: Er - yes, but let's not waste time. I'll get those ships loaded - then over the seas to London Town!

ALL: To London Town!

(MUSIC 52. Peal of bells starts.)

BLACKOUT (Close traverse tabs. Fly in Sceen 11 frontcloth, if used. Peal continues and fades into a single chime for the beginning of Sc. 11.)

## PART II

### Scene Eleven - BACK IN LONDON

(Frontcloth or tabs. Scene 2 cloth could be used again. Tabs to begin. Enter ALICE R., very poor, with a basket containing bunches of lavender.

<u>MUSIC 53</u>   'LOVE IN LAVENDER')

ALICE
    Won't you buy my sweet lavender,
        Two bunches for one penny?
    Won't you buy my lovely lavender?
        Makes your linen very sweet.

    I have laid my love in lavender,
        I have put my love away;
    And as sweet as lovely lavender
        My love will always stay.
    In Spring and Summer of the years
        My love for him has grown;
    Now I have laid my love away,
        For my love is all his own.

    When dreaming in the dark of night
        His voice again I hear;
    Then I awake to morning light -
        But never is he near.
    One day I know he'll come again,
        One day our love will bloom;
    Then I'll take my love from lavender,
        From sweetly scented lavender.

    Won't you buy, etc.

(Open traverse tabs. Enter FITZWARREN L., also very poor, with tray of pedlar's goods slung from his neck. Card on front of tray - 'FITZWARREN'S STORES'.)

FITZWARREN
Ribbons, bootlaces, hair pins. All cheap.
(To ALICE.)   Would you like to buy some ribbons, madam? They're really very pretty, look - oh no, they're the bootlaces.

ALICE
Father, it's me, Alice.

FITZWARREN
(peers closely at her)   Oh, so it is. Really I

can't see a thing since I had to pawn me glasses. I was so hoping you were a customer, too, I haven't had a customer all day.

ALICE　　　　　Oh, poor father.

FITZWARREN　　Ah me, to think this is all that's left of Fitzwarren's Stores. (Sighs.) Have you done well today, my dear?

ALICE　　　　　(as brightly as she can) Oh, I've had some customers, Father.

FITZWARREN　　Ah well, of course, you're prettier than I am. How many bunches have you sold?

ALICE　　　　　Er - quite a few.

FITZWARREN　　How many's that?

ALICE　　　　　(after a little pause) Two.

FITZWARREN　　Oh.

ALICE　　　　　Well, it is twice as many bunches as yesterday. Don't lose heart, Father. Something's bound to turn up soon. The 'Saucy Sal' is sure to be back in port any day now.

FITZWARREN　　(shaking head sadly) No, no, my dear. The 'Saucy Sal' was wrecked nearly a twelvemonth ago.

ALICE　　　　　Wrecked - the 'Saucy Sal'?

FITZWARREN　　Oh, what an old silly I am. I was keeping that a secret from you. I didn't want you to know that there was nothing - left to hope for.

FITZWARREN　　All lost, I'm afraid. Poor old Sarah and Jack.

ALICE　　　　　And Dick?

FITZWARREN　　Dick?

ALICE　　　　　Yes, Dick Whittington.

FITZWARREN　　That scoundrel, that thieving rascal! Ah well, he's dead now, poor fellow. Dry your eyes, my dear, I believe there are some customers coming.

(MUSIC 54. EMPEROR's WIVES enter L., followed by EMPEROR smoking his hookah, the bottle part

|  |  |
|---|---|
|  | of which is held by last WIFE.) |
| EMPEROR | Wifeys, halt! |
|  | (They halt R.C.) |
|  | Stand at ease, stand easy. |
|  | (They do so. MUSIC 55. Enter JACK L., also smoking a hookah, the bottle part of which is held by ULUL.) |
| JACK | Wifey-to-be, halt! |
|  | (ULUL halts and JACK draws on hookah, almost choking himself. FITZWARREN and ALICE approach EMPEROR.) |
| FITZWARREN | Ribbons for the ladies, sir? |
| ALICE | Lavender, sir? Please buy some lavender. |
| FITZWARREN | (approaching ULUL) Hair-pins, bootlaces, very useful for - er - yashmak strings. |
| ULUL | Ah, London Bazaar, me think. |
|  | (EMPEROR busies himself looking at their goods.) |
| SARAH | (off L.) Jack! Empie! Ulul! I do wish everybody wouldn't run ahead so. (Enters L., very richly dressed.) Ah, there you all are. Jack, if only it hadn't disappeared, we could have taken them to Fitzwarren's Stores. |
| EMPEROR | (pointing to card on FITZWARREN's tray) But this is Fitzwarren's Stores. |
| JACK, SARAH | What? |
|  | (The four see each other properly.) |
| SARAH | Fitzy! |
| JACK | Alice! |
| FITZWARREN | Sarah! | (Together.)
| ALICE | Jack! |
| SARAH | We've been looking for you all over the place. |
| JACK | What happened to you? |

| | |
|---|---|
| ALICE | Father lost all his money when the 'Saucy Sal' was shipwrecked. |
| FITZWARREN | I heard you were all drowned. |
| JACK | No, we were all saved. |
| SARAH | And now we're all bursting with money! |
| ALICE | All saved! You mean - Dick too? He was saved? |
| JACK | Haven't you heard? |
| SARAH | He's the richest of the lot. |
| JACK | He's a knight. |
| JACK, SARAH | He's the Lord Mayor of London! |

(Enter CAPTAIN and MATE L. as superior pair of flunkeys.)

| | |
|---|---|
| CAP and MATE | Make way for his Worship, Sir Richard Whittington, Lord Mayor of London. |

(MUSIC 56. Enter DICK L., very resplendent.)

And his Excellency, the Town Clerk.

(MUSIC 57. Enter TOMMY very proudly, L., wearing gold collar.)

| | |
|---|---|
| FITZWARREN | Well, bless my soul. |
| DICK | Mr Fitzwarren! Alice! |
| ALICE | Oh, Dick! Dick, is it really you? |
| DICK | Alice, my love. I've searched all London for you. |

(They embrace.)

Alice, do you remember before I went away I promised I'd ask you to be my wife?

| | |
|---|---|
| ALICE | Yes, Dick. |
| DICK | Will you, Alice? Will you? |
| ALICE | Oh, Dick, things are so different now. Father's so poor and - and - |
| DICK | But I've wealth enough for all of us. Mr Fitzwarren, will you give me your daughter's hand in marriage? |

| | |
|---|---|
| FITZWARREN | No. |
| OTHERS | No? |
| FITZWARREN | I may be poor, but I'd rather that than let my daughter marry a thief. Come, Alice. |
| | (Turns to go. ALICE sorrowfully turns to follow. OTHERS all exchange looks, then JACK steps forward.) |
| JACK | Stop. |
| | (FITZWARREN and ALICE stop.) |
| | Dick's not a thief. I stole that money. |
| DICK | You, Jack? ⎫ |
| OTHERS | What? ⎬ (Together.) |
| | (CAPTAIN and MATE move to either side of JACK.) |
| CAP and MATE | That's right, and we helped him. |
| JACK | I was jealous of Dick, and I hoped that when he was kicked out Alice would fall in love with me. |
| FITZWARREN | Disgraceful! Call a beadle, somebody! |
| DICK | No, wait! I was the one most hurt by Jack's theft. But he's had the courage to confess, and as he did it for love of Alice, I freely forgive him. |
| JACK | Thank you, Dick. ⎫ |
| OTHERS | Bravo! ⎬ (Together.) |
| DICK | (to FITZWARREN) Will you not add your pardon to mine? |
| FITZWARREN | Well, if you put it like that - yes. And of course, if you still want to marry my daughter, I shall be very pleased. Take her with my blessing, which is about all the dowry I have to offer, unless you'd like some ribbons, bootlaces or hairpins. |
| DICK | If you'll let me, sir, I'll make good all your losses and we'll open a new store - Fitzwarren and Whittington. |
| FITZWARREN | That's a very good idea. I should be a bit lonely with Alice married and nothing to do. |

| | |
|---|---|
| SARAH | I tell you what, Fitzy, you shall marry me. I've been looking for a husband for years. |
| EMPEROR | Oh. I was rather thinking of asking you myself. |
| SARAH | You're doing all right as it is. |
| ULUL | And me will marry Jack-Jack. Me already bought ring-ring. |
| DICK | Splendid. Then let's go to the Guildhall and celebrate a triple wedding. |
| ALL | Yes - to the Guildhall! |
| CAP and MATE | (moving R.) Make way for the Lord Mayor. |
| | (The exit R.) |
| EMPEROR | Wifeys, march! |
| | (MUSIC 58. They exit R., followed by him.) |
| JACK | Wifey-to-be, march! |
| | (JACK and ULUL exit R.) |
| SARAH | Hubby-to-be, march! |
| | (FITZWARREN and SARAH exit R.) |
| DICK | (offering ALICE his arm) My love. |
| | (MUSIC 59. DICK and ALICE exit R.) |
| TOMMY | (looks after them a moment, then adjusts collar, has a quick cat-lick, looks off L. and 'meows' softly. Pause. He 'meows' again a little louder and jerks head to indicate 'come on'. Enter THOMASINA L., an elegant lady cat with large ribbon round her neck tied in a bow.) |
| BOTH | Meow! (They rub noses.) |
| | (Close traverse tabs. Fly out cloth. MUSIC 60 'PUSSY DUET'. A dance in which TOMMY woos THOMASINA, who is rather coy at first. At end of dance he gives her his arm, turns a beaming wink on Audience and they exit R. MUSIC 61 and traverse tabs open to reveal Scene 12.) |

## PART II

### Scene Twelve – SIR RICHARD WHITTINGTON'S RECEPTION AT THE GUILDHALL

(Full stage. Rich decor. Rostrum at back with steps down in C. Wings L. and R.
CHORUS enter from L. and R. on rostrum in pairs. Each pair meets in C. of rostrum and comes D.C. to take their bow. They then split and back away to form diagonal lines L. and R. The Principals follow a similar procedure, forming diagonal lines in front of CHORUS. FAIRY from R., backing R. and KING RAT from L., backing L.: EMPEROR from R., backing R.: ULUL from L., backing L.: FITZWARREN from R., backing R.: CAPTAIN from R. and MATE from L., both backing L.: IDLE JACK from L., backing L.: SARAH from R., backing R.: THOMASINA from R. and TOMMY from L., both backing R.
<u>MUSIC 62.</u> Fanfare. ALL turn in as DICK from R. and ALICE from L. meet in C. of rostrum.)

| | |
|---|---|
| ALL | Hurrah! |
| | (DICK and ALICE move D.C. to take their bow. PRINCIPALS move down into a straight line with them. CHORUS move up onto rostrum.) |
| DICK | Good friends, we bid goodbye to you, <br> For all our tale is told right through – <br> I have both fame and fortune won. |
| ALICE | And I a husband – that's more fun. |
| SARAH | So now you can go home to sup <br> And then to sleep |
| | (JACK falls asleep.) |
| ALL | (with Audience) Hey! Jack, wake up. |
| | (JACK wakes.) |
| DICK | But ere we take our final bow <br> Tommy would like to say – |
| TOMMY | Meow. |
| | (<u>MUSIC 63.</u> 'THE LORD MAYOR'S SHOW' (Reprise.) |
| ALL | Our story's told, it's very old; <br> The past is over and gone; |

But the moral's plain
If you will turn again,
   Like our Sir Richard Whittington.

CURTAIN

## FURNITURE AND PROPERTY PLOT
### PART I

**Scene One**

Set on stage:    Practical bell pull and knocker on door of
FITZWARREN's store D.L.
Cup on chain attached to cut-out pump U.C.

**Off R.**

| | |
|---|---|
| Notice 'DO NOT DISTURB' | JACK |
| Large prop alarm clock fitted with practical spring. | " |
| Prop hammer. | " |
| Wheeled shopping basket with walking stick handle, fitted with prop engine. On the front of the basket is a large card with letters 'V.L.'. Numerous parcels in the basket. | SARAH |
| 2 soda water syphons. | " |

**Off L.**

| | |
|---|---|
| Large prop hour glass. | FITZWARREN |
| Flower with detachable petals. | JACK |
| Jug. | SARAH |
| Long rope attached to small 4 wheeled trolley. On front of trolley a ship's wheel and on back a prop anchor attached to the trolley by a rubber line. | CAPTAIN & MATE |
| Beauty Queen-type broad ribbon, worded on back 'MISS STEAK, 1401'. | SARAH |

**PERSONAL**

| | |
|---|---|
| FITZWARREN | 2 pairs of spectacles and a bowler hat |
| SILVERCHIME | Wand. |
| DICK | Bundle on stick containing 2 crusts of bread. |
| CAPTAIN & MATE | 2 cutlasses with detachable handles. |

**Scene Two**

**Off D.R.**

Flower (from Sc. 1.)

## Scene Three

Set on stage:  Shop bell attached to door U.C.
String of onions hanging to R. of door.
Tailor's dummy set R. of door.
Jar of various coloured lollipops on high shelf on shop wing L.
Shop wing R., with clock face painted on it and movable hands.
R.C. a cash desk on which is FITZWARREN's bowler hat, a prop banana and a large cash register with practical drawer containing change for £5 note.
Spring on back of drawer, catch to hold in drawer.
Under desk, a large safe in which is a bottle of Guinness.
L.C. a counter running up and down stage.
On counter: Large packet labelled 'BICARB', side of bacon, string of sausages, pad of paper and pencil, telephone, a pair of scissors and a movable cheese (piano wire attached to cheese and threaded through a hole in the counter and operated by SARAH.)
DICK's bundle U.S. of counter.
Set of kitchen steps behind counter.
Dust pan and brush for SARAH.

### Off R.

| | |
|---|---|
| Large account book. | FITZWARREN |

### Off U.C.

| | |
|---|---|
| 2 £5 notes | CHORUS GIRL |
| Money bag | FITZWARREN |
| DICK's purse and a tool bag containing prop road drill, prop stick of dynamite (edible rock) with fuse attached, large box of matches. | JACK |

### Scene Four

Check DICK has his bundle.

### Scene Five

Set on stage:  Leaves scattered on rostrum. One leaf with thin nylon line attached, running offstage.

### Off R.

Car — This is made on a frame dividing into 2 parts and running on 8 concealed trolley wheels and held together by a catch on the inside.
The back, D.S. side and bonnet are filled in and painted to represent the bodywork. The U.S. side may be left open. Detachable outside brake on D.S. side. Bonnet flap made to lift up.
Powder bulb fixed to painted radiator, operated by JACK inside car bonnet, for steam effect. Steering wheel and practical horn on car.
Picnic basket on luggage rack at back of car.
In basket: Table cloth, 3 plates (2 unbreakable and 1 made from old 78 gramophone record, heated in oven to soften, shaped over a plate and painted. Administered with a sharp tap this is quite harmless), long prop French loaf, prop ham, custard pie, trifle and blancmange made from whipped up and variously coloured shaving soap.

## PART II

### Scene Six

Set on stage: Plank of wood set against R. wing.
Rudder set against gang plank.

### Off R.

2 large kit bags and a large box, marked 'KWELLS'. — FITZWARREN

Large scroll of paper. — ALICE

### Off L.

2 marlinspikes. — CAPTAIN

### PERSONAL

MATE — Pipe and matches.

### Scene Seven

<u>Off D.R.</u>

| | |
|---|---|
| Sheet and pencil | SARAH |

        This is the sheet with the words of song sheet ('CATAWAUL' No. 39) written clearly on it but it should look like a sheet when she brings it on.

### Scene Eight

Set on stage:   Ship's wheel with small hooter attached C. The wheel must be practical and detachable. Line and sinker U.R. at back of rostrum.
Telescope set on brackets U.L. at back of rostrum. Telescope has a T.V. aerial on the front and a flexible insert so that it bends when extended.
Fishing rod U.R. on rostrum.
3 mops in front of wing L.

<u>Off L.</u>

| | |
|---|---|
| Long rope. | JACK and SARAH |

<u>PERSONAL</u>

| | |
|---|---|
| MATE | Small bell on a chain. |

### Scene Nine

<u>Off D.R.</u>

| | |
|---|---|
| Large prop fish | TOMMY |
| Large bag containing: Large knitting needles, large packet of grass seed, large flower pot with skein of raffia set inside, 5 pieces of music used in Scene 10. | SARAH |
| Port hole labelled 'SAUCY SAL' | JACK |

<u>Off D.L.</u>

| | |
|---|---|
| Grass skirt | SARAH |
| 3 spears | ALI, ABDUL and FAKRASH |
| Scimitar | CASSIM |

Prop coconut made of soft material to be thrown on from as high as possible.

PERSONAL

| | | |
|---|---|---|
| TOMMY | Bulb filled with water and rubber tubing going from it to R. ear of costume to squirt jets of water. | |

Scene Ten

| | | |
|---|---|---|
| Set on stage: | Cushions piled on dais L.C.<br>Hookah (practical) on dais.<br>Sword on wing L. and on wing R. | DICK & KING RAT |
| | Punkah | MUSTAPHA |

Off L.

| | |
|---|---|
| Low trolley on castors with simulation of dish and cover, made of painted canvas on a wire frame, large enough to cover the crouched form of KING RAT. | CHORUS |

Scene Eleven

Off D.R.

| | |
|---|---|
| Flat basket with bunches of lavender. | ALICE |

Off D.L.

| | |
|---|---|
| Tray of pedlar's goods: ribbons, bootlaces, hairpins, etc. Card on front of tray 'FITZWARREN'S STORES' | FITZWARREN |

Check EMPEROR has his hookah.

| | |
|---|---|
| Hookah (practical). | JACK |
| Gold collar | TOMMY |

# EFFECTS PLOT
## PART I

**SCENE ONE**

| | | |
|---|---|---|
| 1. | Loud alarm clock bell | Off, as convenient. |
| 2. | Loud motor car engine | Grams or tape. |
| 3. | Sudden burst from engine | "   "   " |
| 4. | Birdsong | Off L. |
| 5. | Jangle of door bell | "   " |

**SCENE THREE**

| | | |
|---|---|---|
| 6. | Telephone bell | Off, as convenient. |
| 7. | Road drill, very loud | Grams or tape. |
| 8. | Hissing of fuse burning (best done vocally, amplified by mike if necessary.) | Off R. |
| 9. | Small pop (pop-gun) | "   " |

**SCENE FIVE**

| | | |
|---|---|---|
| 10. | Motor car engine | Grams or tape. |
| 11. | Car backfiring (blank pistol shot) | Off, as convenient. |
| 12. | Wasp buzzing (can be done vocally, amplified by mike if necessary) | "   "   " |
| 13. | Buzzing | "   "   " |
| 14. | " | "   "   " |
| 15. | " | "   "   " |
| 16. | " | "   "   " |
| 17. | " | "   "   " |
| 18. | " | "   "   " |
| 19. | " | "   "   " |

## PART II

**SCENE EIGHT**

| | | |
|---|---|---|
| 20. | Ship's bell sounding eight bells | Off, as convenient. |
| 21. | Ship's bell sounding four bells | "   "   " |
| 22. | Glass crash (bucket of broken glass flung into second bucket) | Off R. |
| 23. | Thunder (thunder sheet) | Off, as convenient. |
| 24. | " | "   "   " |
| 25. | Wind noise (wind machine) | "   "   " |

## SCENE NINE

26. Loud splash (log dropped into zinc
tank of water)                                Off R.


## MUSIC PLOT

1. Overture.

### PART I

## SCENE ONE

| | | |
|---|---|---|
| 2. | 'LONDON', Opening Chorus | CHORUS |
| 3. | IDLE JACK's entrance music | ORCHESTRA |
| 4. | 'BUSY LITTLE FELLOW' | JACK and CHORUS |
| 5. | ALICE's entrance music | ORCHESTRA |
| 6. | 'I'D LIKE TO FALL IN LOVE' | ALICE and CHORUS |
| 7. | SARAH's entrance music | ORCHESTRA |
| 8. | 'AS YOUNG AS YOU THINK' | SARAH |
| 9. | KING RAT's music | ORCHESTRA |
| 10. | FAIRY's music | ORCHESTRA |
| 11. | TOMMY's music | ORCHESTRA |
| 12. | DICK's entrance music | ORCHESTRA |
| 13. | 'SOMETHING'S BOUND TO HAPPEN' | DICK and TOMMY |
| 14. | CAPTAIN and MATE's entrance music | ORCHESTRA |
| 15. | 'YOU'RE SO LOVELY' | DICK and ALICE |
| 16. | 'THE LORD MAYOR'S SHOW' (Continue, ORCHESTRA only, as link to next scene.) | ENSEMBLE |

## SCENE TWO

| | | |
|---|---|---|
| 17. | KING RAT's music, reprise 9 | ORCHESTRA |
| 18. | KING RAT's music, reprise 9 | ORCHESTRA |
| 19. | 'DIRTY WORK' (Continue, ORCHESTRA only, as link to next scene.) | CAPTAIN, MATE and JACK |

## SCENE THREE

| | | |
|---|---|---|
| 20. | 'DIRTY WORK' fast tempo version | SARAH |
| 21. | 'AWAY, AWAY!' (Continue, ORCHESTRA only, as link to next scene.) | ENSEMBLE |

## SCENE FOUR

| | | |
|---|---|---|
| 22. | KING RAT's music, reprise 9 | ORCHESTRA |
| 23. | FAIRY's music, reprise 10 | ORCHESTRA |
| 24. | CAPTAIN and MATE's music, reprise 14 | ORCHESTRA |
| 25. | Reprise 13, sadly | ORCHESTRA |
| 26. | Reprise 13, gaily (Continue as link to next scene.) | ORCHESTRA |

## SCENE FIVE

| | | |
|---|---|---|
| 27. | Motor car music | ORCHESTRA |
| 28. | 'THIRTY-TWO BAR ROCK' | SARAH, JACK and FITZWARREN |
| 29. | FAIRY's music, reprise 10 | ORCHESTRA |
| 30. | TOMMY's music, reprise 11 | ORCHESTRA |
| 31. | FAIRY's music, reprise 10 | ORCHESTRA |
| 32. | Ballet and finale | FAIRY and CHORUS |
| 33. | Entr'acte | |

## PART II

## SCENE SIX

| | | |
|---|---|---|
| 34. | 'HEAVE HO!' | CAPTAIN, MATE and CHORUS |
| 35. | 'SOMEBODY LOVING ME' | JACK and ALICE |
| 36. | 'STAY THIS LOVE' | ALICE and DICK |
| 37. | 'OUT TO SEA' (Continue, ORCHESTRA only, as link to next scene.) | ENSEMBLE |

## SCENE SEVEN

| | | |
|---|---|---|
| 38. | KING RAT's music, reprise 9 | ORCHESTRA |
| 39. | 'CATAWAUL' (Continue, ORCHESTRA only, as link to next scene.) | SARAH, TOMMY and AUDIENCE |

## SCENE EIGHT

| | | |
|---|---|---|
| 40. | 'QUIET CONTENT' | DICK |
| 41. | Hornpipe production number | ENSEMBLE |
| 42. | 'WE WISH WE HADN'T GONE TO SEA' | CAPTAIN, MATE, SARAH and JACK |